AF378796

The Battle of Stepney

The **Battle** of **Stepney**

The Sidney Street Siege:
Its Causes and Consequences

COLIN ROGERS

ROBERT HALE · LONDON

ISBN 0 7091 9146 4

Robert Hale Limited
Clerkenwell House
Clerkenwell Green
London EC1R 0HT

Photoset by
Kelly Typesetting Limited
Bradford-on-Avon, Wiltshire
Printed in Great Britain by
St Edmundsbury Press, Bury St Edmunds, Suffolk
Bound by Weatherby Woolnough, Northants

Contents

PART IV   LEGAL PROCESS

Illustrations

CREDITS

Illustrations reproduced by permission of the following: British Library, 1, 8 (Ordnance Survey, 1916); Corporation of London Records Office, 4, 5; *Illustrated London News*, 3, 9, 14; Press Association, 10, 12, 13; BBC Hulton Picture Library, 7; Syndication International, 2, 6, 11.

Plans

Acknowledgements

Over the years a great many people have gone out of their way to help me with this book. My warmest thanks go to them all.

I would like to record my particular gratitude to Peter (Plantagenet) Somerset Fry, who gave me sound practical advice and encouragement when the work was in its infancy, and to Donald Rumbelow, who took a magnanimous view of our relationship as competitors and also rendered some valuable assistance. I am no less grateful to Audrey, my wife, who rallied me on countless occasions when supplies of perseverance were running low.

The staffs of what were then known as the Reading Room, the State Paper Room, the Map Room and the Newspaper Library of the British Museum often smoothed my path beyond the call of duty, as also did those of the Corporation of London Records Office and the Public Record Office in Chancery Lane. I am obliged too to the authors and publishers of the books I have quoted from or otherwise referred to in my text, details of which will be found on the appropriate pages and in the index.

My account of the legal proceedings arising out of the case is based on the day-by-day summaries which appeared in *The Times*, the *Daily Telegraph* and the *Morning Post* (the two latter newspapers of course later became one). I am heavily indebted to them, and still more so to the ubiquitous army of Fleet Street reporters, many of them anonymous, who covered every other aspect of the case so exhaustively. But for all these tireless gentlemen of the Press there could have been no book and I have given them and their papers due credit whenever possible.

C.R.

To
AUDREY, NICK,
HETH and MIKE

Introduction

The murder of three policemen by Eastern European immigrants in Exchange Buildings, a tiny cul-de-sac just inside the City of London, on a windy night in December 1910, and the spectacular sequel which occurred in Sidney Street, Stepney, seventeen days afterwards, have fascinated me for more than forty years. The British usually immortalize their more colourful law-breakers in an impressive assortment of volumes, and I was frequently puzzled during this long time by the scarcity of accurate and detailed information about the two events. So far as I can discover, this is the first independent full-length study of them ever undertaken.

Now, having spent six years working on it, I am a wiser—though certainly not a sadder—man. Nobody who, unlike myself, writes books for a living could take the time needed to wade through the morass of hearsay, conjecture, exaggeration and contradiction that surrounds the case without imperilling his solvency. Uncovering and restoring Pompeii must have presented similar difficulties.

Moreover, the case contained such a profusion of unconventional ingredients that it makes highly untypical reading as a real-life murder story. Most of the celebrated crimes of the past, for example, culminated in full-scale trials, and it is of course mainly upon what transpired at these that professional writers draw. Besides being exceptionally complex, unwieldy and (in several fundamental respects) ill-defined, the Exchange Buildings–Sidney Street affair declined to abide by this helpful tradition. Although none of its principals ever stood in the dock, however, it did give rise to six separate legal proceedings which ran to forty-eight sittings in all. It is upon the mountain of evidence given at these by more than a hundred witnesses that this book is based.

Contemporary accounts proved a valuable source of colour but called for very careful scrutiny. Bombarded as we are today with news from reputable origins, it is difficult to realize how different things were only two generations ago. In those days accurate news was a scarce commodity available only in newspapers and magazines, often deeply embedded in highly charged comment and supposition masquerading as fact, to the few who were habitual readers. What little the majority of the common people knew, or fancied they knew, about events outside their personal experience reached them mostly by word of mouth from relatives and friends. Rumour had a field-day when the events were as dramatic as these.

In addition, the Great Britain that awaited George V's Coronation was a nation of steadfast, even passionate believers—in God, King, Country and Empire, the paterfamilias, stern punishment for wrongdoers and many other time-honoured principles now in fashionable eclipse; and men can do strange things to a story so closely bound up with cherished convictions. *Autre temps, autres mœurs*; this was a heroic era in which cold facts were seldom permitted to challenge warm faiths.

More often than not, the general social context of a memorable crime has little bearing on it. The Exchange Buildings and Sidney Street episodes, however, were so much a product of their particular time that the story would not be complete without some account of the various social and political factors which contributed to them. As to the particular social context, no such story seems to me to have been satisfactorily told unless the action, no matter how fascinating, is kept subordinate to the humanity concerned in it. I have therefore included information of purely 'human interest'—for instance, about the pitiful straits to which a number of innocent people were reduced by the Sidney Street incident—such as crime stories normally pass over.

No common felonies before or since can have aroused more widespread controversy. I have described this phenomenon in some detail. A particular reason for this extraordinary impact on public opinion was the extent to which the Liberal Administrations of the previous five years had polarized the political philosophies of Left and Right. With Labour support, Herbert

Henry Asquith and his colleagues were busy preparing much of the ground later occupied by Beveridge and the Welfare State; it was the obduracy of the House of Lords in the face of their Radical policies that led to the second General Election of 1910 taking place only a matter of days before the Exchange Buildings murders were committed.

Feelings ran high, and political debates and speeches were often extremely acrimonious. This 'People versus Peers' election returned a Commons of virtually the same composition as before, thereby confirming Asquith's mandate and intensifying the antagonism of those who feared and hated him and his works. The Exchange Buildings affair, supposedly the outcome of a decadent Radical solicitude for aliens, criminals and Jews, came as a heaven-sent opportunity to release such pent-up emotions.

History keeps on obstinately repeating itself, and most of the main bones of contention – immigration law, for example—are all too familiar to us today. Reactions were strong at every level of society, from the newly disembarked refugee to the King himself. Other important reasons for this were the effrontery that characterized the crimes and the dismay of an intensely law-abiding public at the two London police forces' poor showing in their Herculean efforts to master the situation. In fact, not a single major development arose from their detective skills; all resulted from lay assistance of one kind or another.

Over the previous thirty years the harsh oppression and anti-Jewish discrimination prevailing in Tsarist Russia (together with the keen nose of the shipping companies for a lucrative traffic) had brought literally millions of Eastern European refugees to Britain. Most of these unfortunates had passed on to the New World, but colonies of them had sprung up in Britain, particularly in the East End of London. So long as these aliens knew their place, kept in it and behaved themselves, as the overwhelming majority did, their presence was little more to the average Briton than a token of his magnanimity. Exchange Buildings and Sidney Street woke him to some disturbing realities: they were present in far greater numbers than he had realized; not all of them were properly grateful for his hospitality, some—unkindest cut of all—did not give tuppence for the British way of life, and a few were even peculiarly vicious criminals.

These immigrants, mostly young and Jewish, mirrored all the rebellious political attitudes of their downtrodden fellow-countrymen at home. Some were for forcing the appointment of a government in their country which would have the interests of the masses as its first concern; others went so far as to advocate a life unfettered by government of any kind. The full spectrum of revolutionary aspiration and activity in Eastern Europe was so wide that generalization is dangerous, but, broadly speaking, the latter were described as 'anarchists' (with the added distinction of a capital 'A') and many of the former had banded together as Social Democrats.

As the Anarchist label was freely attached to any individual who repudiated government and the rule of law, whether he acted on his beliefs or not, so-called Russian Anarchists came in an infinite variety of strengths. Most immigrants from that part of the world contented themselves with theorizing and gradually put the ugly past behind them, but some worked, or continued to work, for the revolutionary solution of their choice; prominent amongst these were the militant Anarchists, mostly engaged in plotting desperate deeds for commission abroad or turning out virulent propaganda, and the more moderate and responsible Social Democrats.

As with customs, so with environment. Between them, the Luftwaffe and a burgeoning social conscience have drastically altered most of the mean streets in which the drama unfolded. The tenements in Exchange Buildings and the scene visited by Winston Churchill amid the stirring events of 3rd January 1911 have long since disappeared. But one factor at least links then inexorably with now: what £1 bought in the years immediately preceding the First World War costs us £15–£20 today.

Imposing a semblance of shape and order on such a sprawling tale was not unlike getting the pastrycook's wife into an hour-glass corset. Part I, which begins by introducing all but two of the principal Eastern European characters, tells of what happened between the afternoons of Friday, 16th December 1910, and Monday, 2nd January 1911. Part II records events in Sidney

Street that night and the following day, and Part III deals with their repercussions in the Press at home and abroad, in Parliament, in Sidney Street itself and elsewhere. Part IV summarizes, as a juryman might have seen them, the course (after 3rd January) and conclusion of all the legal proceedings not concerned with Sidney Street alone.

It should be added that much of the evidence given at sittings after 3rd January has been used in compiling Parts I and II and that, to assist coherent narration, some deliberate misfiling has taken place in Parts III and IV.

One last but most important point: until now it has been customary to take for granted the guilt of the five men accused of complicity in the Exchange Buildings crime. I consider this assumption unwarranted and have tried, particularly in Part IV, to bring out the substance of the evidence for and against all eight defendants, so that the reader may judge their guilt or otherwise for himself.

Prolonged study of this period, so very recent but so very, very different from our own, has left me with a deep and enduring affection for it. It is my earnest hope that the story that follows will enable the reader to share this sentiment with me.

C.R.

Pinner
Middlesex

Villains and Suspects

The following Eastern Europeans were known or suspected by the police to have been implicated in the Exchange Buildings crimes. The names by which they are normally referred to are shown in capitals. All but two are introduced in the opening chapter.

Men

Yourka DUBOFF. Real surname, Laiwin. (Yourka=George.)

Josef (or Osip) FEDOROFF.

George GARDSTEIN, otherwise Carl Garstin. Real name believed to be Poloski, or Poolka, MOROUNTZEFF. (Variations: Murontzeff, Mourimitz, Maurivitz, Milowitz, Morintz, Morin etc.) Held two passports in other names.

Karl HOFFMANN, otherwise Masais or Chochol. Held passport in name of Trokhimchik.

Joe LEVI or 'Josef the Jew'; see Max SMOLLER.

PETER THE PAINTER. Peter Piaktow or Piaktoff (believed to be his real name), otherwise Schtern. Sometimes called 'the Frenchman'.

Jacob PETERS or Peter, otherwise Jacob Colnin or J. Peters-Colnin. Introduced in Chapter 8.

John ROSEN. Real surname, Zelin.

Max SMOLLER, otherwise Joe LEVI, sometimes called 'Josef the Jew'.

Josef (or Yoshka) SOKOLOFF. Sometimes called Peter. (Yoshka=Josef.)

Fritz SVAARS, otherwise Trokhimchik.

Women

Luba MILSTEIN.

Rosie (Sara Rose) TRASSJONSKY (Trechjanskaya), otherwise Selinsky.

Lena (or Nina) VASSILEVA. Introduced in Chapter 24.

PART I

Outrage

1. A Round Dozen

The heavy rain of the morning had passed and a blustery wind was springing up as Nicolai Tocmacoff, who had decided to call on Fritz Svaars, turned south out of the Commercial Road into Grove Street. Street hawkers had resumed their pitches, the pavements were drying out rapidly, and litter was being blown about. A tram clanged past him on its way to Aldgate.

Much worn but elaborately cared for, Tocmacoff's clothes did their best to conceal his precarious financial position. Like many another Russian immigrant in London, he was leading a hand-to-mouth existence. At home in Moscow province he had made a living as a musician, but he was unable to do so here. For a spell he had survived mainly by playing the balalaika in clubs on Sundays, but now, five months after his arrival, he was about to take work as a tailor's seam-presser with a fellow expatriate in Spital Square.

To the tall, narrow-chested young musician it seemed that one of the most promising friendships he had yet struck up in London was with Fritz Svaars. Through Fritz and his immense circle of friends might well come an early return to his chosen livelihood. It was Fritz who had brought him engagements at the Anarchist Club in Jubilee Street, now unhappily closed, and Fritz who had recently presented him with a sorely needed pair of boots. Fritz not only radiated confidence but could always be relied upon to show an exuberant appreciation of his art; Tocmacoff was carrying with him now his mandolin and (in his head) several new songs for his patron to hear.

Grove Street (now called Golding Street) was a dingy, narrow thoroughfare lined by the ubiquitous East End cottages of the period, rudimentary dwellings comprising four rooms—'two-up-and-two-down'—and kitchen. The front ground-floor rooms of many of these tiny homes, almost exclusively occupied by immigrants, had been converted into business premises; next to no. 59, at which Tocmacoff now knocked twice, was a second-hand-furniture shop.

The occupier of no. 59 was Mark Katz, a Jewish journeyman baker from Kieff in Little Russia who went to work in the evenings and spent much of the daytime sleeping and, being also a pigeon-fancier, tending his birds; neither he nor his wife Lizzie was familiar to Tocmacoff, although he had visited their house several times. Fritz or Luba normally came down and let him in, but this time a little girl—one of the three Katz children—opened the door to him.

The date was Friday, 16th December 1910, and the time about 1 p.m. The musician stepped into the cramped, ill-lighted passage. Immediately to his right was the door to the Katzes' bedroom. Ducking several times to avoid lines of washing, he climbed the steep, unbanistered staircase and glanced inquiringly into the back room.

It was empty but for Rosie, who was preparing food. The others were in the front room, she told him, and he could go on in.

In the corner of the front room directly opposite the door stood its most prominent feature, an untidily made-up single bed; the iron bedstead was of unusually ornate design and had been painted green. A yellowing but still garish paper covered the walls, on which were pinned several crudely coloured lithographs. The other principal furnishings, a table in the middle of the room and a desk, were old and rickety. Cigarette-ends and spent matches littered the fireplace and the bare, long-unscrubbed floor.

Fritz Svaars welcomed his unexpected visitor in his usual boisterously bonhomous manner. He pressed a glass of wine on Tocmacoff and fell in enthusiastically with the suggestion that the new songs should be heard. The musician was used to Fritz's tall and cultured fellow-lodger Peter (or 'the Frenchman', as some of Fritz's friends called him) being less forthcoming; looking beyond Fritz's blond head and square, curiously thrust-forward shoulders, he was reassured by the other man's amiably interested glance.

Peter was in conversation with Yourka Duboff, whom Tocmacoff also knew, but the musician could not say afterwards what they had been talking about. A pallid, neatly-dressed young Lett with a luxuriant crop of carefully brushed-back light-brown hair, Duboff was later to give his own account of the discussion.

A house-painter, he was in a worse predicament than Tocmacoff, having been discharged on the previous Monday, 12th December. He knew that Peter, also a painter, had decorating commitments both at "a house where emigrants stayed" and for an amateur theatrical performance in Spitalfields on Boxing Day, and that the former (which would bring payment) called for more than a single worker. He visited Peter on 13th December and again on 16th December to inquire after the two jobs and today presented him with a small water-colour he had just painted as a sweetener, the other man (who himself dabbled in oils) having shown an interest in this hobby of his.

Duboff's painting was a wooded landscape, and before talking to Peter, he showed it to Luba; not knowing it was ear-marked, she asked him to give it to her. When he left to catch a 17 bus back to his lodgings in Shepherd's Bush, he handed Peter a slip of paper bearing his name and address.

The fourth person in the front room when Tocmacoff entered was Luba. Rosie lived alone in Settles Street, just across the Commercial Road, and was thus only a constant visitor, whereas Luba was Fritz's woman and lived with him in the back room.

The musician, who understood the situation, did not see it as odd that the woman visitor should prepare food in the back room while the woman resident sat in what normally served as the three lodgers' parlour. A twenty-six-year-old Jewess of strongly Slavonic appearance, sallow, dark-eyed and raven-haired, Rosie was handicapped physically by deformities of the left hip and right shoulder and mentally by an obsessive determination to be needed and to belong. At present it was her ardent desire to be needed by the debonair Peter, to belong to him and be fully accepted as a member of the group.

The two women worked as skirt-finishers for Luba's brothers at their workshop in Eagle Place, off the Mile End Road. Their close association meant a great deal more to the intense, possessive Rosie than to the other woman. Luba was seven years Rosie's junior, a fair, fresh-complexioned Jewish working-girl whose uncomplicated good nature and pliability lent her a pale charm.

Next to arrive was Fedoroff, one of the three Josefs. It would have been difficult to mistake Fedoroff's high cheekbones, flowing moustache, piercing eyes and tangled hair; Tocmacoff, by this time fingering his way through the songs, recognized him at once and noticed him in animated conversation with Fritz. A thirty-year-old native of St Petersburg and the oldest of the afternoon's visitors, Fedoroff was a mechanic. His plight was in turn worse than Duboff's; he had been out of regular employment since his dismissal from a Hackney locksmith's in mid-November.

Again, Fedoroff subsequently explained the reasons for his visit. Fritz had undertaken to help him find work, he said, and had invited him to call on this particular afternoon to hear the outcome of an approach to one of his friends. In the event, it transpired that the approach had not yet been made. They discussed Fedoroff's job-prospects generally.

Other men turned up after Fedoroff, but the musician had become too immersed in his songs and their reception by his expanding audience to observe them at all closely. He was acquainted in some degree with them all. The only two chairs being occupied by this time, several of the men grouped themselves round Peter's bed. Josef the Jew, straight-backed but inclined to corpulence, with his long nose and thick lips, sat on one side of it, mixing colours while Fritz watched; the third Josef (Sokoloff), tall, black-haired and swarthy, leaned against one of the bedposts; Duboff was also sitting on the bed, and Fedoroff lying on it. Peter was playing draughts with the barber, another Lett, whose name (John Rosen) Tocmacoff did not know or remember.

Rosen stated later that his visit to 59 Grove Street was made at the suggestion of Karl Hoffmann, another member of the group. Hoffmann, a sailor in summer and a paperhanger in winter, duly saw Fritz and was seen by Tocmacoff.

Tocmacoff also noted the presence of a twelfth person, a

handsome, aloof young man who looked like an intellectual but moved like an athlete. The others, several of whom knew him as 'Poolka', lost something of their easy informality when under his notice. He and Fritz talked together in Lettish for a while. As Fritz circulated amongst his friends, his bellowing laugh was frequently heard; the reticent, soft-voiced Poolka laughed rarely, and his laughter did not reach his eyes.

Fritz invited Tocmacoff to stay for dinner, but the musician declined. After agreeing to play for Duboff and Fritz at Duboff's lodgings in Shepherd's Bush on Sunday, he left his mandolin behind on the table. Nobody who was later required to describe events at this gathering said they had heard anything unlawful discussed by anyone.

2. A Very Strange Noise

Connecting Bishopsgate Street (and Liverpool Street station) with Aldgate High Street, Houndsditch was in the early 1900s almost as notorious for the tangle of lanes and alleys that surrounded it as it was famous for the keen prices of its toy-factories and fancy-goods importers. In 1908 some of its more prosperous residents and traders had petitioned, unsuccessfully, for the ancient but now not-so-honoured name to be changed. The Houndsditch area, observed *The Times*'s leading article on Monday, 19th December 1910, "is the great receiving ground of the poorest class of aliens from Eastern Europe" and "harbours some of the worst alien anarchists and criminals who seek our too hospitable shore".

Other newspapers made similar comments. As often as not, notices were in French, German or Yiddish; English was fast becoming an unknown tongue. The area had become "the natural lair of the foreign gaol-bird", *The People* declared on Sunday. The idea of such a situation having arisen within the medieval confines of the City of London and scarcely a stone's throw from some of its most venerable institutions was naturally manna to newspapermen in full cry.

Halfway along Houndsditch on its north-east side stood nos. 120 and 119. No. 120 was occupied by Max Weil, a German Jew who traded there as a fancy-goods importer under the name of Isenstein. Weil lived upstairs with his spinster sister and a serving-maid. No. 119, next-door to the north, accommodated the unpretentious lock-up shop of a goldsmith, silversmith and jeweller called Henry Samuel Harris. The rear of the ground floor and two upstairs floors, all wholly separate from Harris's shop, were rented to a lace-merchant named Rosenfeld. Nobody lived in this building.

Next door again at no. 118 was a dairy, and beyond this another shop, Lipman's. On the far side of Lipman's was a site for another shop and a corner site, on both of which rebuilding was in progress.

This was the corner of Cutler Street, a short street leading north-eastwards into Harrow Alley (now Harrow Place) and on into Middlesex Street, better known as Petticoat Lane. About twenty-five yards along Cutler Street on the right was a blind alley containing twelve tenements and ending in a packing-case repository. The name of this brief, drab cul-de-sac (of which the side of a public house called 'The Cutlers' Arms' and tenements 1 to 6 constituted the left flank, and a house and tenements 12 to 7 the right) was Exchange Buildings. The turns into Cutler Street and again into Houndsditch amounted to 180 degrees, and, although the relative party walls were not precisely aligned, 11, 10 and 9 Exchange Buildings thus stood back to back with 118, 119 and 120 Houndsditch respectively.

Exchange Buildings having originally accommodated a market, the ground-floor frontage of each tenement was constructed to allow the centre section to be taken out. Later on, when the market was discontinued, the front had been closed in with matchboarding to a height of 4 feet and three windows placed above. Topped by a line of thirteen small panes, these windows ran almost the entire length of the ground-floor room. Shutters were provided to put over them at night.

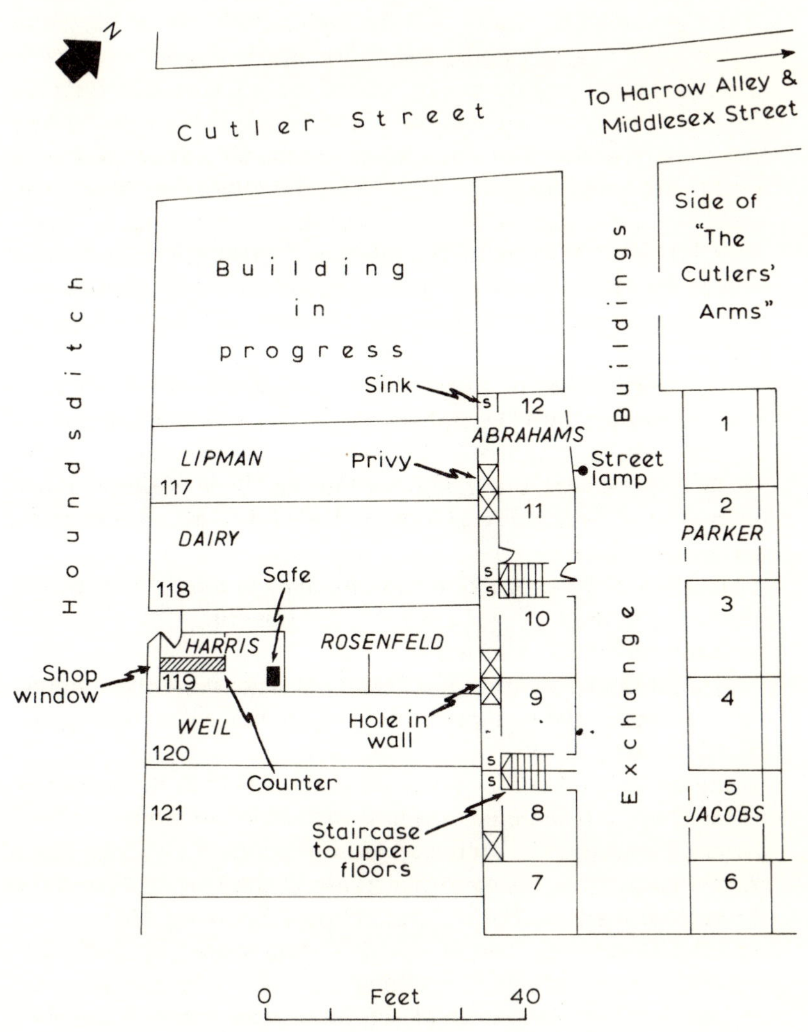

Cutler Street
To Harrow Alley &
Middlesex Street
Houndsditch
Building in progress
Sink
S 12
ABRAHAMS
LIPMAN
117
Privy
11
Street lamp
DAIRY
118
Safe
S
S
10
HARRIS
119
ROSENFELD
Shop window
9
Hole in wall
Exchange
WEIL
120
S
S
Counter
121
8
Staircase to upper floors
7
Buildings
Side of "The Cutlers' Arms"
1
2
PARKER
3
4
5
JACOBS
6
0   Feet   40

The tenements had one room only on each of their three floors and were built in pairs, parlour to parlour. Nos. 11 and 9 had their real street door on the left and a simulated one on the right; access to the ground-floor room was through a doorway on the right, just inside the street door, and to the upper floors by a narrow staircase facing that door. The side of the staircase adjoining the ground-floor room was boarded, and beside this, at the back of the room, was the door into a yard. On the far side of these back yards, the same length—14 feet—as the tenements and 3 feet wide, were the rear walls of the Houndsditch buildings.

Each back yard contained an enclosed privy at one end and a sink at the other. These conformed to the same mirror principle, nos. 11 and 9 having their privy on the right and their sink on the left.

To Max Weil, letting himself into 120 Houndsditch at about 10 p.m. on Friday, 16th December 1910, a typical Sabbath seemed to have begun. He had just visited a friend. The weather was mild for the time of year, but the high winds had been tiresome. It had been a busy week; he was looking forward to his supper and a comfortable bed.

His sister, however, came running to meet him. One glance at her face and the face of the servant girl hovering behind her put such thoughts out of his mind.

"Thank God you are come," said his sister fervently. "Something very strange is happening, and the noise it is making you should hear!"

The noise had first been noticed at about 9.15 by the servant in the kitchen. It resembled "drilling and sawing and the breaking-away of brickwork", Weil said later in court. It could be heard more distinctly in his counting-house at the rear of the ground floor. Weil suspected some kind of house-breaking. He went out into the street and, finding Harris's shop locked up, looked in through the window. Everything was precisely as usual, the electric light above the great safe in a rear corner of the shop making it clearly visible to passers-by. He called at nos. 118 and 121. The noise was audible in both, and this decided him. He walked back along Houndsditch and, rounding the corner into Bishopsgate Street, spoke to a City policeman.

It was now about 10.45. 344C Constable Piper was not alarmed. He had had reports before from residents in this part of Houndsditch about unusual noises at night. If Mr Weil would return home and leave his front door ajar, Piper said, he would follow shortly and investigate.

Piper arrived at no. 120 a few moments later. Weil took him to the counting-house, and they listened to the noise for several minutes. It seemed to the constable to come from the back of the party wall between nos. 120 and 119. On the second floor there was a back bedroom with a window overlooking Exchange Buildings (but not the yards); Weil led Piper upstairs to this, and they looked out. Nothing unusual was to be seen or heard. When they came down again, the noise was continuing. Piper decided to go round to Exchange Buildings.

Most of the tenements in the cul-de-sac were unoccupied as dwellings. Of nos. 9, 10 and 11, only no. 11 showed a light above its green ground-floor shutters. Before calling there, Piper made inquiries of the families at no. 12 and no. 2, both residents of many years' standing. He learned little. The occupants of no. 11 were foreigners who had only moved in less than three weeks before, kept themselves to themselves and were rarely seen except at night.

Piper then approached no. 11 and rapped on the door.

The manner in which it was opened, both instantly and not freely, aroused his suspicions at once, as did the manner of the man who opened it. Piper took him for a Russian. He decided to pass the interview off.

"Is the missus in?" he asked.

"No, she is gone out," the man answered in broken English.

"Right," said Piper, "I'll call again."

The time was 11.10. With the violent, gusty wind and it being the Sabbath, Piper noticed as he walked back to Houndsditch how few people there were about and how quiet the neighbourhood was. The blind end of Exchange Buildings was in darkness. Later he also recalled seeing a man (whom he described as about 5 feet 7 inches, pale and fair-haired) standing on the other side of Cutler Street looking down Exchange Buildings. As the constable came near him, this man moved off towards Borer's Passage, a footpath leading from the northern end of Cutler Street into Devonshire Square (and from there to Bishopsgate Street).

In Houndsditch Piper met two uniformed colleagues, Constables 395C Woodhams and 406C Choat. It was decided that Piper should go to Bishopsgate Street police-station for assistance while Choat remained near no. 119 and Woodhams kept an eye on Exchange Buildings. From shortly after 11.10 onwards, the cul-de-sac was thus under continuous police observation.

Piper located 39C Sergeant Bentley and reported the situation. Bentley called upon a fourth uniformed constable, 399C Smoothey, and the trio, being now in the northern part of Bishopsgate Street, set out for Houndsditch by way of Devonshire Square and Borer's Passage. When they reached Cutler Street, Bentley instructed Smoothey to maintain observation there.

The sergeant then accompanied Piper on another visit to Weil's premises. Bentley, who possessed an unusually resonant voice, was speaking as they entered the counting-house; the noise ceased abruptly. It could again be heard at the back of the dairy, however, when they called there.

"Leave it in our hands," Bentley told Weil as they left him. "We will see to it."

Back in Houndsditch the illuminated safe seemed invulnerable and far removed from the mysterious sounds. They had been joined by two plain-clothes patrolmen, Constables Martin and Strongman, and Bentley had sent Choat round to Exchange Buildings to accompany Woodhams. Harris lived some distance away in Curtain Place; the sergeant instructed Strongman to return to the police-station and ask the night-duty inspector to summon him with his keys.

Bentley then took Martin round into Exchange Buildings, where they talked with Choat and Woodhams and debated which of the tenements backed directly on to Harris's premises. Martin indicated no. 9, which was still in total darkness, but Bentley thought it was too far round. They then went back into Houndsditch, where they met two more sergeants, 33C Tucker and 35C Bryant, and Strongman, who had duly delivered his message. It was 11.30.

Seven uniformed men and two plain-clothes patrolmen were now on hand. All were equipped with the regulation truncheon, the constables in plain clothes carrying theirs in their coat pockets. The next move was clearly another call at 11 Exchange Buildings. Bentley decided to leave Piper in front of 119 Houndsditch and Smoothey in Cutler Street as at present. Piper watched Bentley, Bryant and Martin, Tucker and Strongman disappear round the corner into Cutler Street.

Two or three minutes after their departure, he heard a rapid succession of sharp reports. The Metropolitan Railway emerged from underground at the Cutler Street end of Harrow Alley, and detonators were sometimes used on it, but these reports were too many and too near. He ran to the corner of Cutler Street. About 20 yards away, Smoothey was struggling against Tucker's weight, trying to ease him to the ground . . .

At a minute or two after 11.35, standing at his open front door, Max Weil saw Piper pulling the ambulance alarm outside his house. He asked what the reports had been.

''Some of our men are shot,'' Piper replied.

''Shot?'' echoed Weil blankly. ''How many?''

''Five or six, I think.''

That so terrible a thing should occur—and on the Sabbath! Where were suitable words in English for such a calamity to be found? Making shocked sounds, Weil gently closed the door.

3. The Hole in the Wall

Directly it was evident that the shooting was over, the tiny cul-de-sac became a bedlam. People poured out of the 'Cutlers' Arms' and neighbouring houses. Horror-struck men and hysterical women ran in every direction, shouting in many tongues. The landlord of the 'George and Dragon', another nearby public house, blew a police whistle repeatedly. Choat had fallen just outside the front door of no. 12; Mrs Abrahams, of the family living there, rushed out and fell heavily over him.

Within minutes many other City policemen began to arrive. Some still wore their off-duty mufti; others, from the Bishopsgate Street section-house, were only partly dressed or had tried to dress as they came. It was soon established that all five uniformed men in Exchange Buildings had been shot, but the surrounding pandemonium made their evacuation extremely difficult.

Tucker, who had collapsed just round the corner from the cul-de-sac, was carried across Cutler Street and laid on the opposite pavement. He was obviously at the point of death. Smoothey unbuttoned his tunic and found a wound immediately over the heart. As he staggered from Exchange Buildings, an onlooker had called out to Tucker "Are you shot?" and he had gasped "Yes." This was the last word he ever spoke.

Smoothey now tended him as best he could while some brandy was fetched from the 'Cutlers' Arms' and they awaited an ambulance. At Piper's urgent request, however, a man and woman gave up their taxi-cab in Houndsditch; the two constables put Tucker into it, and Smoothey accompanied him to the London Hospital in the Whitechapel Road, where he was found to be dead.

Bentley, the first man shot, was lying on his back just inside the front door of no. 11 with his head on the pavement. Helped by another policeman, Martin carried him into the narrow carriage-way and opened his tunic. He had been hit in the neck and right shoulder and was unconscious. The Bishopsgate Street motor-ambulance was instructed to take him to St Bartholomew's Hospital at West Smithfield.

Choat's condition suggested that he had offered resistance to the assailants. No less than six bullets had struck him, three in the trunk and three in the left thigh, calf and foot; two of the latter had passed right through. Having disposed of Tucker, Piper came to Choat's aid, and he was placed in a hand-litter. Chief Inspector Hayes arrived at this point and spoke to him. The constable's lips moved in reply, but in the hubbub it was impossible to make out what he said. Woodhams, severely injured in the left thigh, had fallen in the carriageway not far from Choat; the two men were removed to the London Hospital.

Bryant was the only victim still on his feet. Wounded in the left arm and (as he learned subsequently) the chest, the sergeant fell down but later found himself, dazed, leaning against the wall of no. 10. He made some remark to Martin, who was standing nearby, and was taken by a Constable Jones into the 'Cutlers' Arms'. He talked incoherently but was soon sufficiently recovered to walk to a doctor's surgery in nearby Goring Street. From there he went on to St Bartholomew's Hospital, where the second wound was discovered.

One of the City force's three superintendents, Detective Superintendent Ottaway, was on the scene before midnight. It cannot have taken long to deduce that more than one person had made the affray and that they had done so expressly to make escape possible. Numerous witnesses were testifying freely to anyone who would listen about the flight of at least one assailant, and, with the victims attended to, a full-scale attempt might have been expected to pick up the trail and discover where the villains went to earth.

This course was not followed. The fact that the criminals were sure to have fled beyond the City boundary onto the territory of another force, the H (Whitechapel) Division of the Metropolitan Police, no doubt influenced the decision. Instead a cordon was thrown round Exchange Buildings, the crowd inside dispersed and a massive search mounted. Where necessary, untenanted houses and shops were entered by running ladders up to their first-floor windows. Harris's premises and the new building on the Houndsditch–Cutler Street corner were also minutely examined. The operation lasted until nearly four o'clock but failed to flush out any criminals.

This meticulous locking of the stable door at least provided the police with plentiful evidence of the felony they had prevented. The following summarizes Detective Superintendent Ottaway's account of what he found, as given later on in various courts:

> The first house in Exchange Buildings which I entered was no. 11. The door leading into the ground-floor room had been removed. In this room a two-flame ceiling gas-pendant gave a bright light. A large fire was burning in the fireplace. In the centre of the room,

which also contained a gas-stove, a chest of drawers, an armchair, a couch and three ordinary chairs, stood a table spread with a kind of white quilt on which lay some rough eatables. All the chairs were upholstered.

One of the front window-panes had a bullet-hole in it. There was a corresponding hole in the shutter outside. From their position, the shot that made these holes appeared to have been fired through the doorway of the room from the stairs. In the ceiling of this room were two further bullet-holes close together, the shots responsible having apparently been fired from near the doorway and slanting upwards.

In the first-floor room, which was in darkness, were a bed and bedclothes, a table and a chair. This chair and the three downstairs seemed to belong to a set. There was a hole in the ceiling where one of the two bullets had entered it. The second-floor room was empty. On the staircase between the first and second floors was a window looking on to the yard. This was open.

In the yard of no. 10, which was unfurnished and unoccupied, I found a kind of stallboard such as a costermonger's barrow has. This had been so placed that the roof of the privy (and the privy of no. 9) could be reached by using it as an improvised ladder. Once on the roof, it would be easy to drop into the yard of no. 9. There was in fact evidence that persons had passed from the yard of no. 11 to that of no. 10, and then on to no. 9 in this way.

The street door of no. 9 possessed two locks, one old and the other new. In one corner of the ground-floor room a gas-pipe ran vertically to within a foot of the ceiling. Fixed to this pipe with black tape was a 63-foot length of india-rubber tubing which extended through the back door into the yard. Other discoveries here consisted of four sheets of asbestos; two wooden boxes, one 48 inches by 12 inches by 13 inches with a carpenter's drill in it, the other 23 inches by 15 inches by 18 inches and empty; a bag of sand; some recently mixed mortar and two candles.

Outside, leaning against the sink, was a long iron oxygen-cylinder fitted with a regulator and an appliance for attaching tubing to it. Nearby was a large roll of brown paper. Inside the privy was a quantity of brick debris and a collection of tools—a carpenter's brace, three diamond-pointed drills (to which clung particles of brick and mortar), a chisel, three crowbars and a special combined wrench and cutter.

In the wall of the privy on the Houndsditch side, brickwork had been cut away to make a diagonal hole some 24 inches by 20 inches. The hole was about 9 inches deep and had in one place penetrated to the matchboard lining of the back room of 119 Houndsditch.

Scale: 1 inch = 210 feet

The Houndsditch area, from the 1916 Ordnance Survey.

The jeweller's shop in Houndsditch.

10 and 11 Exchange Buildings.

The superintendent also discovered two empty bottles in a cupboard under the stairs at no. 11. These bore discernible fingerprints, and Scotland Yard's fingerprint department took them over a few hours later.

Superintendent Ottaway's evidence was complemented by that of a Constable Grimes: "On the table in the ground-floor room of 11 Exchange Buildings I found a double blowpipe with about 7 feet of flexible metallic tubing and 7 feet of india-rubber tubing attached to it; also a pressure-gauge, a screwdriver, a file, a clothes-brush, a right-hand kid glove, an electric pocket-lamp, two wax candles and a paint brush." A Detective Constable Beechey found another right-hand kid glove on the chest of drawers.

It was apparent that 11 Exchange Buildings had been occupied openly for domestic purposes and no. 9 clandestinely for felonious ones. Nobody living in the cul-de-sac associated no. 9 with any new occupier.

Many witnesses' descriptions of the affray were elaborately embellished, but Bessie Jacobs, seventeen-year-old daughter of the family living at 5 Exchange Buildings, provided Saturday's London *Evening News* with a sober account. Hearing loud voices in the street, said Bessie, she went to her front door. A police sergeant was standing at the door of no. 11 with other policemen behind him. He knocked and requested admittance. After waiting about two minutes, he pushed the door open and started to go inside. Almost immediately a shot rang out, and he staggered backwards. A young man with a pistol then rushed out into the street. The policemen began to retreat; he stood and fired four times at one of them, until the policeman fell. After this the man ran out of Exchange Buildings, his pistol still in his hand, and disappeared round to the right. He was "rather tall", was wearing an overcoat and a light hat and was not the man Bessie had known as the occupier of no. 11. She had not seen anyone else leave the tenement.

Other witnesses told similar stories. No. 2, immediately opposite no. 11, was the home of Ada Parker, her parents and brother. On hearing the first shots, the Parkers thought the wind had blown down a chimney. By the time realization had dawned and they had run upstairs to the unshuttered first-floor window, three policemen were lying on the ground, and a fourth was staggering away towards Cutler Street. A young man who was in the 'Cutlers' Arms' with a friend thought "something had gone wrong with the mechanism of a passing taxi-cab". His more worldly companion speedily disillusioned him. "No," he exclaimed, rising excitedly, "that's a shooter!" They rushed to the door and emerged just as Tucker was shot.

One of these young men was Harry Jacobs, Bessie's brother. Although his account in Monday's *Daily Mail* contained several basic inaccuracies, it gave a graphic idea of the fate that had overtaken Choat. After Tucker had passed him, Harry said,

> I saw from the corner of Exchange Buildings Constable Choat struggling with a man. The burglar evaded the constable's clutch at his right hand and, boring close in upon the policeman, emptied his pistol.
>
> A second man ran out from no. 11 and fired point-blank at Choat's back. Both the struggling men staggered, and at last Choat fell.

Harry had helped Constable Jones take Bryant into the 'Cutlers' Arms'; and it was in answer to Harry's inquiry that Tucker spoke for the last time.

None of the Exchange Buildings tenements possessed a rear exit. One of the criminals seemed to have made his getaway alone and ahead of his associates, who had left in a bunch a minute or so later. It is odd that Bessie and Harry Jacobs and several other onlookers did not recall seeing them escape as well. None of the police survivors was ever to admit seeing even one man do so.

However, at least one occupant of the 'Cutlers' Arms' remembered that "some men" rushed past, and this was confirmed by three witnesses nearby. One was Isaac Levy, manager of Salmon & Gluckstein's tobacconist's shop in Walthamstow; the others were George Smith and John Richardson, employees of a contractor to Stepney Borough Council.

Isaac Levy, who lived in Goulston Street (alongside Petticoat Lane), was an upright and God-fearing man but of a neurotic disposition. On 16th December he left his shop as usual shortly after 11 p.m. and caught a Liverpool Street train. His walk home from Liverpool Street Station took him through Borer's Passage and along Harrow Alley. As he approached the Cutler Street end of Borer's Passage at about 11.35, he heard a succession of shots from the Exchange Buildings direction. He broke into a run and, on entering Cutler Street, found himself face to face with three men and a woman.

In view of his very positive identification of all three men within the week, an interview with Levy recorded in Monday's *Daily Mail* is interesting. He had "caught but the slightest impression" of the party, the *Mail* reported him as saying; he doubted whether he would be able to recognize the men again. Two of them had worn bowler hats and the other a cap; two revolvers had been levelled at him, and he had been ordered not to follow. The party then ran off through Harrow Alley, and he went to Exchange Buildings.

Giving evidence later, Levy said that two of the men had the third between them and were holding him up and helping him along. The woman was close behind them. All four were running and seemed excited.

After stopping for a moment at the cul-de-sac, Levy went to Bishopsgate Street police-station. Here he told Chief Inspector Hayes about the situation in Exchange Buildings but did not mention his earlier encounter with the armed fugitives. Asked why not, at Guildhall later on, he replied, "I didn't know how the firm would take such a thing. They don't like me to be implicated in a matter like this." He then returned to Exchange Buildings and helped evacuate the victims. The following afternoon he changed his attitude, paid the police a further visit and described the encounter in a detailed statement.

George Smith was flushing gullies in Cobb Street, immediately across Petticoat Lane from the further end of Harrow Alley. At about 11.40 he saw four men, one of whom was being supported by the others, coming from the Harrow Alley direction. He had just heard some noises "as of boards being blown down". He particularly noticed how white in the face the man being helped along was. He had a dark moustache, Smith said, and was wearing a cloth cap and a blue Melton overcoat. The four men moved briskly into nearby Wentworth Street, where Richardson was working and saw them. He and Smith both concluded that the disabled man was drunk. The party turned out of Wentworth Street into Goulston Street, which led into Whitechapel High Street.

Although the two contractor's men had been working within 300 yards or so of Exchange Buildings, and in the easterly direction which the fugitives were known to have taken, the police did not approach them; Smith heard soon afterwards about the affray and, realizing the significance of what they had seen, told an inspector in Cutler Street about it.

Constable Choat died at 5.20 on Saturday morning.

This was the first occasion within living memory that even one City policeman had been murdered on duty. The protocol involved in enlisting the aid of the Metropolitan Police was complied with; Scotland Yard instructed Superintendent Mulvaney and Detective Inspector Wensley of H Division to give every assistance. Detective Inspector Collins, head of the Yard's fingerprint department, spent two hours in 9 and 11 Exchange Buildings and left with various articles. Both police forces permitted the issue of firearms—old-fashioned and cumbersome Army Service revolvers provided under an authorization of 1883—to detectives searching for the criminals.

To the stolid Anglo-Saxon bobby pounding his beat amid the alien masses of the East End,[1] immigrants from Eastern Europe resembled Chinamen in all looking alike. Now under instructions to keep a sharp look-out for the villains, the meagre official descriptions of three of them gave him little help. One was short and stout, another walked with a slight limp; all were thought to be between twenty-six and thirty. Also sought was ''THE WOMAN: Aged twenty-six to thirty; 5 feet 4 inches; slim build, full breasts; complexion medium, face drawn; eyes blue; hair brown; dress, dark blue, three-quarter jacket and skirt, white blouse, large black hat trimmed with black silk.''

The City force soon learned of an additional strain on its

---

[1] As long ago as 1902–3, when the Royal Commission on Alien Immigration was taking evidence, it had been estimated that 25 per cent of the people who lived in the 2 square miles covered by Spitalfields, Whitechapel, Mile End and Stepney were of alien birth. Within the Mile End Road–Commercial Road–Regent's Canal triangle, the proportion was thought to be much higher—at least 80 per cent at the western (Whitechapel) apex.

resources. Throughout Saturday and Sunday Houndsditch thronged with sightseers. "The narrow thoroughfare was as busy as a fair," Monday's *Daily Express* reported, "and penny-toy merchants took advantage of the crowd to sell their goods." At least a hundred uniformed policemen were employed, it added, keeping everyone on the move and out of Exchange Buildings.

The Lord Mayor and Lady Mayoress visited both hospitals on Saturday morning. Bryant was able to sit up and read the copious accounts of the crime in the early editions of the evening papers; Bentley was conscious and rational, but his legs were paralysed; Woodhams was still badly shocked. Later, speaking about the affray in the Mansion House justice-room, the Lord Mayor implied that a policeman who is suddenly murdered on duty is *ipso facto* a man of the greatest devotion and bravery— a curious thesis wholeheartedly supported by the popular Press.

Thus passed the twelve hours after the affray. The City Police, it seemed, were going to have to pluck their villains more or less out of thin air. A helping hand from Providence was sorely needed.

Against all the probabilities, it came at once.

4. Two Deathbeds

At about 12.30 p.m. on Saturday Scotland Yard and City Police headquarters at 26 Old Jewry received urgent telephone calls from Detective Inspector Wensley. Wensley, who was at H Division's headquarters in Leman Street, had just been advised by the East London coroner that there was a young foreigner dead from a gunshot wound at 59 Grove Street. Grove Street lay about ¾ mile east of Exchange Buildings and was in H Division territory. Led by Wensley and Detective Inspector Thompson of the City Police, a force of about forty Metropolitan and City men descended on the house.[1]

The Katz family was at dinner when its visitors arrived. Mark and Lizzie knew that a man was ill upstairs and that a doctor had been to see him, but neither seemed to have felt any desire, or even moral obligation, to offer assistance. Mark affected a callous indifference both now and later, but the news that the man was dead threw his wife into great confusion. The officers crept upstairs and burst simultaneously into both rooms.

The dead man lay on the narrow single bed facing the door of the front room. He was fully dressed even to his laced-up boots, and a dark overcoat lay untidily at his feet. There was blood on his clothes and the bedding; bloodstained towels were strewn on and around the bed. He had been shot in the back and had obviously died in considerable pain. Detective Sergeant Leeson of H Division, who entered the back room, discovered a woman (Rosie) burning paper in the fireplace. She was about to throw some photographs on the flames, and he wrested them from her; there were five, including one of Luba.

This being H Division's manor but the City Police's case, it fell to Inspector Thompson to give evidence about what had been found at 59 Grove Street. This he did on several occasions. The substance of the rest of his testimony follows:

> Detective Sergeant Richardson of H Division searched the dead man's clothing in my presence. In the pockets were thirty cartridges of 7·65mm calibre, a drill and a key which fitted the new lock at 9 Exchange Buildings. [Constable Strongman, who accompanied the body to Stepney mortuary, also found a pair of welder's goggles.] In addition, Sergeant Leeson and I found in the pockets of his discarded overcoat a fully-charged seven-cartridge magazine clip for a 7·65mm pistol, a further seven loose cartridges of the same calibre, two left-hand gloves, a pair of gas-pliers and a key which fitted the door of 59 Grove Street.
>
> Lodged between the mattress and the palliasse at the head of the bed, Sergeant Leeson found a fully-loaded 7·65mm Dreyse auto-

---

[1] Although nobody could tell what kind of reception might await them, Wensley followed his invariable practice of carrying no arms. A forty-five-year-old Somerset man, he was later to end a remarkable police career as Chief Constable (CID) at Scotland Yard.

matic pistol with, beside it, a second fully-charged magazine clip and a third clip containing six cartridges. In a man's soft cap lying on the table were six ·30 Mauser pistol cartridges and twenty-three rounds of rifle ammunition of other calibres.

Further discoveries included fifty more cartridges in a cardboard box; a cartridge belt; a dagger bearing an obliterated name; a mandolin, a tambourine and a violin; and three paintings, two in oils and one a water-colour signed "Yourka, 15.12.1910". In addition, there was a quantity of written and printed matter and a piece of paper with "G. Duboff, 20 Galloway Road, Shepherd's Bush" written on it.

Amongst other furniture in the front room were two upholstered chairs identical to the four found at 11 Exchange Buildings.

Both rooms were in a state of confusion, as if a hurried search had been made of them.

The medico who had notified the coroner's office of the death was a Dr Scanlan. The police summoned Dr Scanlan to 59 Grove Street, his third visit of the day. From him they learned that the dead man had said his name was George Gardstein.

Gardstein became posthumously one of the most talked-about men in Britain. For reasons which will appear later, his corpse was moved first to the Stepney mortuary in Horseferry Branch Road on the evening of his death, then on to the London Hospital on 19th December and finally to the City mortuary in Golden Lane on 22nd December. There it remained, lying in a special formaldehyde-vapour preservation-chamber with glass windows, until the end of March. On Sunday, while it lay at Stepney mortuary, a City constable photographed the face, the eyes being opened again for the purpose.

An unexpected complication arose when Lizzie Katz announced that the dead man was not one of her lodgers at all but had occasionally called on them. However, Mrs Abrahams's son Solomon, fourteen years of age and succinctly described by the *Daily Telegraph* as a "diminutive but sharp lad", was rushed to the house and recognized him without hesitation as having frequented 11 Exchange Buildings. Whilst at 59 Grove Street, Solomon also saw Rosie and said he recognized her. That he should have been allowed a first sight of Rosie by herself there, rather than in the customary line-up, was of course quite improper.

She was a native of Krenkagrodno in Russia, Rosie told Inspector Thompson at Bishopsgate Street in a guarded first statement, and had been in England four or five months. Although at 59 Grove Street on Friday afternoon, she had not been allowed into the front room. In the evening she and Luba had been to the moving pictures; Luba then returned to Grove Street, and Rosie, after visiting an aunt, joined her in the back room.

At about 12.15 a.m., Rosie continued, some men whom she did not see came upstairs, closed the door of the back room and went into the front one. She and Luba went into the front room shortly afterwards and found Gardstein lying on the bed.

Rosie set to and did what she could for the dying man, uncovering his wound and putting a wet towel on it. Luba became unwell, and Rosie sent her off to her room at 10 Settles Street. Two or three hours later, Gardstein's condition became critical, and he told her to leave him. She went to consult Luba, and they decided to call Dr Bernstein in the Commercial Road. Rosie escorted the doctor to Grove Street, and Luba returned to Settles Street.

Rosie had no money, and Gardstein told her to look in his pockets, where she found a sovereign. The doctor gave her 10 shillings change, which she put on the table. She went back to his surgery with him and was given a bottle of medicine. The tenacious Rosie returned to her patient three more times and was twice more dismissed; the third time—at about 9.30, she thought—he "appeared to be dead".

She and Luba, who had come with her, then returned to her room in Settles Street. They could not make up their minds what to do, Rosie said, and just sat together. She had revisited Grove Street later and burned the letters and photographs "because Luba told me to".

Sergeant Bentley's condition deteriorated during Saturday afternoon, and at about 6.45 it was noticed that he was having increasing difficulty in breathing. He died forty-five minutes later. He had been shot on his ninth wedding anniversary, and his wife, who was at his bedside, was to bear their second child in four days' time.

Robert Bentley, who would have been thirty-eight on Boxing

Day, was a stern but not unkindly man after the simple masculine ethos of the period. 6 feet 3 inches in height and powerfully built, he had joined the City Police just before the Boer War, after several years in the 1st Royal Dragoons; recalled as a reservist, he served at Spion Kop and Ladysmith. Invalided home after a severe attack of enteric fever, he became one of the youngest sergeants ever in the City force. The Bentleys already had a seven-year-old girl.

To the average Briton of the early-twentieth century, the murderer, the detective and the legal luminary were what film stars later became for his children—remote, endlessly publicized figures to hold in awe and fascination. During Dr Hawley Harvey Crippen's long trial in October 1910, he had supped full of pleasurable horrors. Further treats as yet unsuspected were in preparation for him. George Joseph Smith was just embarking on his career as a wife-drowner, bigamist and swindler; Frederick Henry Seddon was disposing of Eliza Mary Barrow's choicer effects prior to disposing of Eliza Mary Barrow; the famous Steinie Morrison case was to be launched on New Year's Day, 1911. In an era in which the public eagerly devours details of violent death and mutilation, the hour perhaps brings forth the men.

The Liberal Government was forewarned of trouble in store by *The People* in its leader on Sunday. Criticizing the despatch of policemen to face armed desperadoes with only their truncheons to protect them, it remarked that

> The Home Secretary [Winston Churchill], who requires 442 constables to guard him at a public meeting, might be supposed to be sympathetic on the point. But then, as a Radical, he is bound to take the susceptibilities of aliens into account, and the police have reason to believe that all these miscreants are foreigners. . . .
>
> So long as the Radicals remain in office, it is hopeless to look for a remedy, since they avowedly administer the Aliens Act with reluctance, inadequate though it is.

Alien immigration was a leading topic for many weeks. (This is examined in Part III.)

It was ironical for the police that, in a week-end of intense activity, the two major developments should both be dropped in their laps at Leman Street police station. A sergeant on duty there on Sunday afternoon was approached by a man and woman. The man introduced himself as Jack Milstein. "This is my sister Luby," he said. "This is the young woman the police are looking for. She lived at 59 Grove Street." The sergeant spoke to Luba, who replied sullenly "I don't know nothing. I don't speak English." Inspector Thompson came and bore her off to Old Jewry, where he and Yiddish interpreter Harry Wagner also obtained an initial statement from her.

It may be noted in passing that Thompson wrote both women's statements out in English and requested their signatures. The women's knowledge of spoken English was small and of written English negligible. Other Russian- and Yiddish-speaking suspects received similar treatment during the course of the case.[2] Whereas Rosie was asked three times to sign and refused point-blank, Luba now complied.

5. The Incurious Doctor

On Monday morning Captain J. W. Nott-Bower, Commissioner of the City of London Police, received a letter from Buckingham Palace. His Majesty had heard the news with the greatest concern and sent the bereaved and the wounded men his sincere sympathy.

Public reaction was immediate and abundant. Messages poured in from City institutions and firms; many sent money. It was announced that the dead men would be accorded a public funeral, including a memorial service in St Paul's Cathedral, on Thursday.

[2] As the Home Office's Administrative Directions on Interrogation and the Taking of Statements were later to comment: "Apart from the question of apparent unfairness, to obtain the signature of a suspect to an English translation of what he said in a foreign language can have little or no value as evidence if the suspect disputes the accuracy of this record of his statement." (Home Office Circular 31/1964.)

The Lord Mayor, who had also received donations, stated that there was no intention of setting up a Mansion House fund, at any rate until the Corporation had decided what official steps should be taken. From a workaday standpoint, this introduced a discordant note. Since the police committee had, as one newspaper put it, "held their last meeting of the year, and the matter cannot be discussed by the whole body for some time", it seemed that someone other than the murdered men's employers would have to avert any immediate financial anxieties.

With Rosie and Luba in their hands and Gardstein's body already identified by several people, the police soon found some firm ground to stand on. About ninety detectives, mostly City men, scoured East End haunts which might be harbouring their quarry. Raids were made on 36 Lindley Street (connecting Sidney Street with Jubilee Street near the Mile End Road) and 36 Havering Street (a turning off the Commercial Road further east), it now being known that Fritz and his fellow-lodger Peter had visited the former shortly after quitting 59 Grove Street and that Peter had then gone on to the latter. Both raids proved abortive, but it has been said that Peter narrowly avoided capture in Havering Street.

Since some of the finds at 59 Grove Street had convinced the City Police that the villains were Anarchists or at least had Anarchist connections, inquiries were also made in Tottenham, scene of the so-called Anarchist outrage of January 1909 (see Appendix).

It was standard practice amongst Eastern European subversives at this time to confound authority by the use of aliases. This brought British detectives, accustomed to home-grown names and the relatively artless behaviour of the home-grown criminal, endless headaches.

The man who had called himself Gardstein was a case in point. No. 11 Exchange Buildings was originally rented by Max Smoller calling himself Joe Levi, and, since Gardstein subsequently occupied the tenement, this was the first surname thought to be his. He was then, rightly, believed to be the man who paid some of the rent for no. 9 but did not originally take it, giving the name of—so the landlord's manager said—Goldstein; he gave his

surname to Dr Scanlan as Gardstein; Rosie knew it as Morount-
zeff; Luba knew it as Maurivitz; Old Jewry later gave it as
Milowitz. He was also known to other East Enders as Garstin,
Morintz and Morin.

As will be seen, much of the confusion arose quite innocently
from varying phonetic renderings. Nor were surnames alone
troublesome. In addition to the Peter who lodged with him in
Grove Street, Fritz had a first cousin in the East End who was
variously called Jacob Peter or Peters, and the tall, dark Josef
(Sokoloff) was apparently known to some associates as Peter—a
factor which led to several major miscalculations.

The City Police issued the following detailed descriptions of
two of the wanted men at midday on Monday:

> FRITZ. Aged twenty-four or twenty-five; height about 5 feet 8 inches
> or 9 inches; complexion sallow; eyes grey; medium moustache,
> turned up at ends; colour of hair on head, fair; nose rather small,
> slightly turned up; chin a little raised; a few pimples on face; cheek-
> bones prominent; shoulders square, but slightly bent forward;
> dressed brown tweed suit, thin light stripes, dark Melton overcoat,
> velvet collar, nearly new; usually wears grey Irish tweed cap, red
> spots, sometimes trilby hat. A native of Russia. Speaks English and
> German imperfectly.
>
> PETER. Surname unknown; known as 'Peter the Painter'. Aged
> twenty-eight to thirty; height 5 feet 9 inches or 10 inches; complexion
> sallow; skin clear; eyes dark; hair and medium moustache black;
> medium build; very reserved manner; usually dressed in brown
> tweed suit, large dark stripes, black overcoat, velvet collar, rather
> old; rather old, large felt hat; shabby black lace boots. Believed to be
> Russian Anarchist. Frequents Club and Institute, Jubilee Street;
> resides Grove Street.

The use of "frequents", the present tense, suggests that Old
Jewry did not know the club had closed. During Monday afternoon the following was added:

> YOURKA. Aged twenty-one; height 5 feet 8 inches; hair and
> moustache, dark brown; dressed in blue jacket suit, grey cap. A
> Russian.

It says a great deal for this period in Britain's history, and the
philosophy to which even her wrongdoers mostly subscribed,

that so little was generally known about the modern firearms used by Gardstein and his associates. The science of forensic ballistics was as yet scarcely born,[1] but the police soon learned that some of the cartridge cases and bullets resulting from the affray could have come from various 7·65mm automatic pistols of common European make, including the Dreyse, and the rest were Mauser ones.

Some six thousand Mauser ·30 self-loading magazine pistols had been sold in Britain since the start of the Boer War a decade earlier; nevertheless, throughout the Exchange Buildings–Sidney Street affair an extraordinary ignorance was displayed about this formidable weapon. The same applies to compact pocket-sized 'automatics' like the Dreyse. Experts were few and popular terms and descriptions often misleading; nearly all so-called automatic weapons, for instance, were actually only semi-automatic, the trigger having to be pulled afresh for each shot fired. The word 'revolver' was habitually used to mean any firearm held in one hand.

Sergeant Bryant's condition worsened on Saturday night, and he was no better on Sunday, when his visitors included Harris the jeweller. It was feared that septicaemia might set in, and his wife and two children were summoned to his bedside. During Monday, however, he showed a definite improvement. Constable Woodhams, a single man, underwent an operation on Sunday to remove the Mauser bullet that had splintered his left thighbone, and he too, despite continuing mental distress, began slowly to recover. He was allowed no visitors.

By Monday morning Fleet Street was well into its stride. Harris's safe, it was generally agreed, had contained about £20,000-worth of jewellery.[2] That the five uniformed policemen had been singled out for attention did not pass unnoticed. The ferocity of the onslaught attracted particular comment: "A savage delight in taking life," said *The Times*, "is the mark of the modern Continental anarchist criminal."

---

[1] Robert Churchill, later to become its best-known exponent in Britain, first gave evidence at the Old Bailey as a firearms expert in the following month. The case, that of Charles Arthur, is referred to later on.

[2] Harris's son testified later that the total value was about £7,000.

As St Bartholomew's Hospital lay inside the City, it was necessary to hold a separate inquest there on Bentley alone. Choat having died at the London Hospital and Tucker *en route* to it, but Gardstein in Grove Street, two further coroners' courts should have held inquests on these three men. Brought about by the anachronistic separateness of the City of London and a law based not on the circumstances of a death but on its location, only chance and the acumen of the East London coroner, Wynne E. Baxter, made some alleviation of this absurd situation possible. Happening to be the coroner appropriate to all three non-City deaths, Baxter was able to have Gardstein's remains transferred to the London Hospital. Even so, the City inquest and the triple East London one had to be held in double harness, complicating matters greatly and wasting a great deal of time and money.

Gardstein's body was brought to the hospital on Monday morning. Many years afterwards Sir Philip Gibbs[3] recorded a macabre conversation arising from this:

> I was lunching for some reason at this time in the London Hospital, when a young man came in excitedly and said:
>
> "We've got him! There was great competition, and he's as handsome as Adonis—a very beautiful corpse."
>
> "Great work!" said my host.

The "great competition" presumably came from the City, which was anxious to gain possession of the body and in fact did so three days later.

The joint inquest on Tucker, Choat and Gardstein had an initial sitting on Monday morning. Baxter, white-haired and wearing his invariable red tie, conducted it in the hospital's small, blue-tiled basement courtroom before an audience composed mainly of police officers.

The personal circumstances surrounding Tucker's and Choat's deaths were almost as inauspicious as Bentley's. Forty-seven years old and with twenty-six years' service, Charles Tucker had already reached his retirement; because of the demands which

---

[3] The well-known author and journalist. Gibbs, later knighted as a war correspondent in World War I, was a special correspondent with the *Daily Chronicle* at the time of the Exchange Buildings murders. This quotation is from his Foreword to *The Mystery of 'Peter the Painter'* by J. P. Eddy, KC (Stevens, 1946), p. 10.

would be made on the force over George V's coming Coronation, he had signed on for a further twelve months only a few weeks previously. Tucker too was married, with children aged seventeen and fifteen. He was a devout Christian and a people's warden at his parish church of St Michael and All Saints in Southwark. He was a sociable man with a deep concern for children, and his employers gave him many child cruelty and neglect cases to deal with. His sympathy with the young was reciprocated: "I dare not tell my little girl what has happened to the sergeant," one of his neighbours confided to the *Evening News*. His coffin lay at St Michael's for some days, visited by many policemen and watched over in turns by the vicar, the curate and a group of personal friends.

Walter Charles Choat, known to colleagues as Joe, was thirty-four and single. Only ten days before his death he had attended his mother's funeral in his native Byfleet. Choat, who was 6 feet 4 inches tall, lived at the Bishopsgate Street section-house; one of the City Police's best billiards-players, he spent much off-duty time improving his game at the table there.

Dressed in deep mourning and red-eyed with weeping, Mrs Amelia Tucker was the first witness. Constable Smoothey followed, and Dr E. H. Rainey, a house surgeon at the London Hospital, testified to the sergeant's being dead on arrival. A post-mortem on Saturday had disclosed two wounds:

> The first bullet track went through the right auricle and left ventricle of the heart, glanced off the right side of the eighth dorsal vertebra, passed through the right lung and right thoral cavity, fractured the sixth rib and was found in the muscle under the skin over the fractured rib.
>
> The second bullet track commenced in the left lateral line of the body 4 inches above the hip bone, grooving the kidney, perforating the colon and small intestine and passing through the fourth lumbar vertebra, near which it was found embedded in the muscle.
>
> Death was caused by the first wound.

Dr Rainey having produced the two bullets, Tucker's case was adjourned and Choat's taken. Dr Rainey stated that on admission the constable was conscious but in shock, having no recollection of what had happened. There were three bullet-wounds in the upper part of his body. He did not complain of pain and was not bleeding externally, though internal bleeding was obviously severe. An operation was decided upon but could not be extended beyond his abdominal injuries. Death occurred two hours later.

A post-mortem had been carried out on Saturday:

> One bullet had entered between the spine and the right shoulder-blade, taken a downward course, fractured the lamina of the seventh cervical vertebra and lodged between the sixth and seventh vertebrae. A second had entered one inch to the right of the tenth dorsal vertebra and was found in the left thoral cavity.
>
> The third bullet, which entered the left loin, had evidently struck a button in doing so. Its track was much more ragged than the others; it had broken up, and the wound was larger and more lacerated. A jagged piece of metal discovered in the peritoneal cavity during the operation was found to correspond with some patent trouser-button fasteners.
>
> The cause of death was heart-failure resulting from loss of blood and shock.

The doctor again produced two bullets, together with a bullet fragment and various pieces of metal.

The court then considered Gardstein's death, summoning Dr John James Scanlan as its first witness. Baxter clearly thought the tall, clean-shaven medical man with the military bearing obtuse and, despite his twenty-odd years as a coroner, sometimes found his asperity impossible to conceal.

The gist of Dr Scanlan's story follows:

> On the night of 16th–17th December I was acting as assistant to Dr Bernstein of 55 Commercial Road. At 3.30 a.m. a woman called through the speaking-tube from the street to my bedroom. I dressed and found two young women at the door. One said "There is a man very bad at 59 Grove Street." They did not tell me what was the matter with him, and I did not ask.
>
> About 25 yards along the Commercial Road one of the women left us without a word and disappeared down a street on the north side [Settles Street, no doubt]. The other woman offered no explanation. There was a light upstairs at 59 Grove Street, but the house was locked up. We knocked repeatedly; I used my walking-stick. Neither of us remarked on the difficulty getting in.

Poloski Morountzeff, alias George Gardstein.

Peter Piaktow or Piaktoff, better known as Peter the Painter.

Detective Superintendent Wensley in February 1923, when he was leading inquiries into the 'poisoned chocolates case'.

Archibald Bodkin KC leaving Stepney coroner's court for the City one on 6th January 1911. He attended sittings of both courts in the morning and a third at Guildhall justice-room in the afternoon.

The Sidney Street area, from the 1916 Ordnance Survey. Richardson Street had been renamed Winwood Street.

When the front door was at last opened, I saw no one. There was no light in the passage. I do not remember anything being said. I lighted a match and followed the woman upstairs. The door of the upstairs front room was ajar, and it was dimly lit by a ceiling gaselier. Nothing was said when we went in. The woman was very silent, but she had very little English.

Before examining the man, I spoke to him in English and asked him his name. I wrote down his reply as George Gardstein. I asked what had happened to him, and he answered, "Three hours ago I was shot by a friend with a revolver in the back by mistake." He was very weak. He vomited blood during my examination and complained of pain in the stomach and abdomen. I concluded that the stomach had been perforated. There was no external bleeding. He asked several times for a narcotic, but I had none with me.

The woman was in the room with us the whole time. I could only converse with her in French; the man spoke very broken English. I suggested he should be taken to the London Hospital, but they would not entertain the idea. [Baxter: "We know why."] They gave no reason. I got back to the surgery at 4.30 and gave the woman some medicine.[1]

I called again at 59 Grove Street at about 11.15 a.m. In the passage I saw two young men. They appeared to be English. I asked them "How is the man upstairs?" They replied that they knew nothing about him. The door of the upstairs front room was closed, and the Holland blinds had been pulled down. The man was dead.

I looked into the back room, but there was nobody there. I then went downstairs, seeing neither the two young men nor anyone else, and left. On my return I telephoned the coroner's officer.

Dr Scanlan had performed a post-mortem at Stepney mortuary on Sunday in the presence of the City and H Division police surgeons and Dr Bernstein:

The body was that of a muscular, well-developed man of about twenty-three. His height was 5 feet 9 inches, and he weighed about 11½ stone. He had long black hair, parted in the middle, heavy dark eyebrows and a light moustache. The eyes were light brown, and the complexion was sallow. The teeth were sound. No marks or deformities whatsoever were found; in fact, he was a perfectly made man. The hands were small and soft and gave no indications of manual work. On the index finger of the right hand was an abrasion which might have been caused by the trigger of a revolver.

---

[1] This was a mixture of nux vomica, belladonna and opium.

The bullet entered 5½ inches from the mid-line of the spinal column between the tenth and eleventh ribs on the left side. It was found lying underneath the skin of the chest wall at a point 2 inches from the mid-line of the chest. After it had entered the body, the bullet went through the left lung in an ascending direction[5] and grazed the apex of the heart, leaving an impression. It pierced the diaphragm and penetrated both walls of the stomach, the spleen and the left lobe of the liver.

Death was due to haemorrhage caused by the bullet-wound.

This bullet too was produced, and Baxter, who had already spoken of its being "inadvisable to go into details more than we can help", announced a long adjournment such as the police had applied for—until 5th January.

6. The Hall of the Friends of the Workers

With the growing conviction in certain quarters—particularly Old Jewry—that the criminals had been Anarchist expropriators came the involvement of the Special Branch, headed by Detective Superintendent (later Sir) Patrick Quinn. This theory, however, was never accepted by the Metropolitan Police, who stoutly denied that the villains were political criminals at all.

The City Police resented these denials. In his memoirs, Nott-Bower referred to the Exchange Buildings felons as "Russian Anarchist burglars" and went on to say:

I have no hesitation in describing as I do this criminal gang, even though (from quarters which might have been supposed to have knowledge) connection with the Anarchist movement has been discredited. . . . The   police   also   had   good   reason   to

[5] Giving evidence later at Guildhall, Dr Scanlan said that the man was clearly in a stooping position when he received the wound, the bullet having taken an upward and irregular course.

> believe . . . that some portion, probably only a small percentage, of
> the proceeds of their crimes was allotted to political purposes.[1]

The disagreement seems to have arisen in the main from differing definitions; the Yard apparently took the view that, if criminals came to police notice not as political assassins or subversives but as common thieves and murderers, any subsidiary connections they might have with such political activities were irrelevant. Since it was never shown that the Exchange Buildings villains had any designs whatever on Britain other than to steal from her property-owners and murder her policemen when balked, this was hardly an illogical attitude; under all the circumstances, however, nor was the Old Jewry one. The Home Office seems to have straddled both police positions, considering that the criminals were Anarchists but had not been acting as such in Exchange Buildings. The two police forces reiterated their conflicting views frequently, causing much public bewilderment.

It was regarded as certain that the wanted men were still in the East End, but the hundred or so detectives continuing the comb-out were looking for the proverbial needle in an alien haystack. Having no Russian or Lettish and virtually no Yiddish isolated them almost as effectively as if they had been transported to Odessa or Riga to track down the criminals there. "In this great foreign city east of Aldgate," 'An Ordinary Man' remarked in the *Daily Mail*, "the English policeman is an uncomprehending foreigner." The *Morning Post*'s Washington correspondent commended the American practice of assigning to the alien districts of large cities detectives of the same national origin as their inhabitants.

The detectives were taking no rest-days and only four or five hours off in every twenty-four, but the time-honoured police expedient of attempting to substitute sheer physical effort for adequate organization and knowledge worked no miracles. Another peculiar difficulty was the great number of floating lodgers in the East End, men who appeared and disappeared at will and in whom no interest was shown provided their rent was

---

[1] Sir William Nott-Bower, *Fifty-Two Years a Policeman* (Edward Arnold, 1926), pp. 231, 232.

paid. Life was hard and minding one's own business the wisest policy. "If there were cries of 'Murder'," one detective remarked, "the people in the next room would merely barricade their doors."

Although their superiors were to be caught unprepared, the searchers themselves knew better. An observation in the *Daily Mail* of Wednesday, 21st December, was prophetic: "If the men have another room similar to the one in which their comrade's body was found in Grove Street, they will by means of their automatic pistols be able, as a detective said yesterday, 'to fill the staircase with dead policemen' unless they are themselves shot down at an early stage."

The City Police disclosure that they believed the wanted men to be Letts and Lithuanians came as no great surprise. The Letts, a people some two million strong centred on the Gulf of Riga, had emerged from serfdom during the previous century. Dominated by German landowners and Lutheran clergy, subjected by the Tsarist Government to periodic attempts at compulsory russification and beguiled by Russian Socialist propaganda, their revolutionary zeal was heightened by nationalist ambitions. Of all the uprisings in Eastern Europe between 1905 and 1908, few produced greater bitterness and violence than those of the Letts in 1905, and the ruthlessness of the two punitive expeditions sent against them by Russia the following year only made matters worse.

The case of their Lithuanian neighbours was similar. These two peoples fathered many of Eastern Europe's most extreme and reckless militants, and although the revolutionary movement's more responsible leaders had formally outlawed expropriation for its debasing effects, there were known to be independent groups of young Letts still engaged in it. To escape oppression and conscription in the Russo-Japanese War that broke out in 1904, thousands of Lithuanians and Letts had fled abroad, many of them to Britain.

The fact that some or all of the criminals were thought to have frequented the Anarchist Club (or 'Hall of the Friends of the Workers', as notices in Russian and Yiddish had proclaimed it) in Jubilee Street gave the police little help. The club had closed down about five weeks before the murders. It had been a popular meeting-place to which, since its opening by Prince Kropotkin (a prominent Russian Anarchist) five years previously, thousands of non-members had paid casual visits.

One of its co-founders, a German bookbinder called Rudolf Rocker,[2] stated categorically that Peter the Painter, Fritz and their cronies might have been callers but were never members. The club was used as a place of propaganda, Rocker said; lectures were given on social problems and prominent men of letters and music. Press reports about it ranged from the humdrum to the horrific. The *Evening News* disclosed that its refreshment-room served no intoxicants, and its reading-room, open to all comers, boasted one of the best supplies of Russian newspapers in London. The police had commended the club's "orderliness and sobriety", the *News* added. The *Daily Express* on the other hand printed an alarming account of the place given by a man who said he had stopped going to it "because the speakers were so violent and I thought the police would come and close it up. They said such things about murdering kings and queens".

Explanations of the club's closure also varied. Charles Martin, the owner of the premises,[3] said that, when he learned that "very advanced views such as he did not approve" were being propagated in the club, he had the lease terminated. The "friends of the workers" were then given £100 to clear out, which they did. Rocker's version, however, was that the Anarchists had left of their own accord; the club was costing too much to run.

A great many people saw the Exchange Buildings affair as an awful warning of what could spring from their particular pet aversion—generally Jews, foreigners and criminals—and a suspected softness of the "Radical cranks and sentimentalists" towards all three. It had given many people a pretext for denigrating Socialism, Labour MP George Lansbury told a meeting,

---

[2] Rocker also edited one of the oldest Anarchist periodicals, the weekly *Workman's Friend*.

[3] Martin, who also owned the building in Jubilee Street at which the *Workman's Friend* was printed, the 'Blind Beggar' public house in the Whitechapel Road and many other properties in the locality, comes into the story again later.

whereas such an outrage was a denial of everything Socialism stood for.

The wanted aliens, the *Daily Mail* asserted, "belong to the class of our demagogues' darlings, the lowest type of foreign immigrant. . .". The same indignant question was asked over and over again: "Who let them in?" Sir Robert Anderson, ex-Director of Scotland Yard's CID, saw one cause of such crimes as "the mollycoddling attitude adopted towards criminals by the Radical Government and a certain so-called humanitarian section of the general public". A vigorous campaign for more frequent use of the cat-o'-nine-tails was soon under way in the *Daily Express* and the *Daily Telegraph*. The political animus behind this movement did not escape the Liberal Press, which let none of its main arguments pass without detailed refutation.

Gardstein's post-mortem having revealed that he was uncircumcized, Dr Bernstein announced "in justice and fairness to the Jewish community" that he was certainly not a Jew. The Hon. Sydney Holland, chairman of the London Hospital, wrote to *The Times* to the same effect. The Chief Rabbi was later to observe that Anarchism and lawlessness were totally incompatible with Judaism.

The Bentley inquest was opened on Tuesday afternoon by Dr F. J. Waldo, the City of London coroner, at his sombre courtroom in Golden Lane. As Mrs Louisa Jane Bentley, in full mourning and heavy with child, passed through the waiting jurors, they raised their hats in sympathy. Mrs Bentley wept as she gave her evidence.

Constable Martin was the second witness. The plain-clothes patrolman, a powerfully built man with a grey moustache, testified in a low, emotionless voice. He too was to give evidence several times. (His version of the affray appears in Part IV with those of the other police witnesses.)

Dr Benjamin Biggar, a house surgeon at St Bartholomew's Hospital, said that, when he first saw Bentley; the sergeant was semi-conscious but suffering from cerebral irritation, struggling and calling out. No operation was contemplated. He was lucid for some hours during Saturday. His legs had become paralysed, suggesting damage to the spinal cord. He died that evening.

A post-mortem had shown that

> There were two bullet-wounds, one in front of the right shoulder-joint and the other in the right side of the neck about one inch from the end of the collar-bone.
>
> The second, third and fourth ribs had been fractured near the spinal column by the first bullet, which was found in the muscles of the back on a level with the fourth rib.
>
> The second bullet had injured the first dorsal vertebra and run through the spinal cord, which was almost completely divided. This bullet was found beneath the skin.
>
> Death was caused by failure of respiration due to laceration of the spinal cord and haemorrhage into and around its membranes, which exerted pressure on it.

The two bullets were produced. Dr Waldo then adjourned until 6th January, the day after the triple East London inquiry was due to resume.

7. A Bright, Happy and Good-Looking Young Man

Inquiries about Fritz Svaars revealed no skulking, black-hearted villain. A Lithuanian cabinet-maker named Grube described him as bright, happy and good-looking. He had first met Fritz, Grube said, at a Socialist meeting where Fritz seemed very well known. Grube soon got to know him better, and in October it was decided to produce a Russian peasant play called *Girts Wilks* on Boxing Night at a hall in Spitalfields.[1]

Fritz, who obviously considered himself no mean hand as an

---

[1] *Girts Wilks* tells of a young Socialist fleeing from the police. A little boy agrees to hide him but, bribed with a watch and chain, reveals his hiding-place. The boy's father appears and, appalled at his son's treachery, shoots him dead. Fritz was to play 'Gamba', a police officer; a wooden sword found at 59 Grove Street was no doubt a personal property for the part.

actor, had embarked on the project with his customary enthusiasm. Two rehearsals had taken place, but a third—arranged for the Saturday afternoon after the murders—had fallen through because of Fritz's absence. The play was now cancelled. Fritz had personally taken a great many tickets for it. Grube believed that his exuberant young friend had Anarchist tendencies, but they had never discussed such things. He had no idea what Fritz's occupation was.

The Lithuanian was shown a picture of Gardstein but did not recognize him.

Another acquaintance who had obviously taken to the seemingly good-natured and open-hearted young man was a Whitechapel grocer who had frequently sent provisions to 59 Grove Street. Fritz, whom he knew jocularly as Fred, had laboriously ordered his requirements in fractured English. The shopkeeper had on several occasions seen him show generosity to paupers and beggars who happened to be in the shop. Fred had extended a hearty invitation to the grocer and his wife to come to the play on 26th December.

From the end of August to the beginning of November, Fritz Svaars had lived at 35 New Castle Place. (New Castle Place, which no longer exists, lay within the western angle of Whitechapel High Street and Commercial Street.) Two months was quite long enough for his flamboyant behaviour to pall, and his landlady there, Mrs Esther Goodman, drew the *Morning Post* a less appealing picture of him and his friends:

> They were a mysterious lot, and we could never fathom what they did or how they lived. The man [Fritz], who was tall and fair and looked either a Russian or a German . . . was visited first of all by a short, square-built man, who seemed to be his greatest friend and was often here. Soon after he took the room, this friend started to do it up thoroughly, although it did not want cleaning at all. He painted all the window-sashes and doors and repainted the walls. . . .
>
> Besides this short man, a number of foreign men and women visited the house at all times of the day and night. One of these was a tall and very handsome man with a pointed beard. He looked like a Frenchman. He was really a distinguished-looking man, apparently quite a gentleman, and something like a doctor. He was exceedingly well dressed, as indeed were they all. They were all foreigners, I

should think Russian, and among the women was one I did not like at all. She never spoke and never looked you in the face.

It is curious that Mrs Goodman should have called Fritz tall and Gardstein, the friend who did the redecorating, short. The handsome caller with the pointed beard could well have put her in mind of a doctor; Peter the Painter was an erstwhile medical student. The silent woman who avoided the landlady's eye was almost certainly Rosie.

By nature withdrawn and solitary, Gardstein showed his desire for Fritz's esteem not only by redecorating the latter's room so painstakingly but in other ways; it was he, for example, who presented Fritz with the set of chairs which later came to be divided between 59 Grove Street and 11 Exchange Buildings. Fritz, however, no doubt disliked poor mixers as much as naturally gregarious people usually do, and his interest in the other man was probably confined to the material benefits promised by association with him. Although the two men had shared a room for several weeks prior to Fritz's stay at New Castle Place, there is no evidence that Gardstein's friendly overtures were ever reciprocated.

They had always seemed to have plenty of money, Mrs Goodman went on. Feasts would be held at which bottles of wine and huge joints of meat were consumed, and afterwards they would make so much noise singing and dancing that the neighbours gathered outside to listen. Fritz used to play a mandolin.

> As to going into the man's room, you could never do such a thing. They used to look at you with eyes like daggers, as if they suspected you were prying into their secrets. Once my little boy went to the door, and he was ordered away very sharply. My charwoman used to clean up his room, and she always had to knock first, to see if he was ready for her. He would often say "Come in an hour's time," and when she went in, there was nothing unusual to be seen in the place. One thing she remarked on, however, was the large number of pens and papers lying about. . . .

Mrs Goodman had understood that Fritz was well off, having been left money by his father in Russia. He had described himself at different times as a sketch-artist and an electrical engineer, she told the *News of the World*. He used to stay in bed nearly all day, go out after dark and return in the small hours. As many as half-a-dozen men visitors, and several women, would often be in his room at once. The neighbours complained, and after a while he was told to leave. He removed his furniture, which was mainly boxes, on a small barrow.

On Wednesday, 21st December, it was announced that the five uniformed policemen concerned in the affray were to receive King's Police Medals. Bryant and Woodhams were promoted sub-inspector and sergeant respectively, as from 16th December, in recognition of their devotion to duty.

At City Wardmotes on Wednesday there was vigorous criticism of the Aliens Act and its administration. A magistrate at the Farringdon Within meeting remarked that he felt sure the desperadoes were foreigners because, when caught by the police, an English burglar normally handed in his checks and said "Right, it's a fair catch." (Laughter and "Hear, hear.") Unless he was drunk or one of the very lowest, he never used firearms or resorted to violence; the Exchange Buildings business was quite uncharacteristic of him. The Castle Baynard Wardmote was told that the families of the two policemen (Sergeants Bentley and Tucker) to be buried at the City of London Cemetery at Manor Park, Ilford, would be presented with the graves, which would be deep enough to be used for near relatives if desired. All interment and other fees would be waived.

Not surprisingly, a controversy also arose about arming the British policeman. Whilst it soon became clear that majority opinion did not favour any general arming, and that amongst its strongest opponents were policemen themselves, it was widely agreed that the weapons issued for dangerous duties ought to be automatic ones. On Thursday evening it was announced that, so far as the Metropolitan Police were concerned, the Home Secretary had decided these should be provided. The welfare of the Metropolitan force was of course the Home Secretary's direct concern.[2] The deputy chairman of the City's police committee,

---

[2] The City of London Police, completely surrounded by the Metropolitan, owe their separate existence to political horse-trading. Sir Robert Peel was obliged to allow the City its own police force in order that his New Police Bill might survive in Parliament.

A. C. Morton, MP, stated that it would "adopt all proper measures" for its own force's protection.

Sara Rose Trassjonsky (or Selinsky) and Luba Milstein were hurriedly charged at Bishopsgate Street police-station at 9 a.m. on Wednesday.[3] The Director of Public Prosecutions had advised the City Police Commissioner that he would be taking up the case. Together or separately, the two women had made a number of statements. Luba had lived with Fritz at 35 New Castle Place for about five weeks, she said, until Peter arrived from Paris; needing more room, they then moved to 59 Grove Street. Four or five men would visit them there, and when they did so, Fritz would not allow her or Rosie into the front room. Morountzeff carried a revolver at all times; Fritz carried one occasionally. Fritz had been in London about six months, Luba thought, and Peter had arrived about two months ago. None of these men was "of Hebrew or Jewish religion".

Each woman faced three charges: being an accessory to the murder of the three policemen by harbouring, comforting and assisting Gardstein, he and other men unknown having been concerned in those murders; assisting the other men unknown; and conspiring with Gardstein and others unknown to break and enter Harris's shop with intent to commit a felony.

On being charged, Trassjonsky replied that she knew nothing of what had happened. Milstein made yet another statement. When she spoke of living with Fritz, Trassjonsky interjected "I live also with a man." As Milstein's statement was being read over to her, Trassjonsky began to cry. Milstein then said "Excuse me, the papers she tore up or burned, it was distinctly by my instructions." "You have nothing to fear. You have done nothing," Trassjonsky told her.

Their sudden appearance at the Guildhall magistrates' court with the City Solicitor, Sir Homewood Crawford, his chief clerk, two wardresses and a covey of policemen caused a minor sensation amongst the many reporters present. Both were neatly, if shabbily, dressed; Milstein wore what the *Daily Express* described

---

[3] Rosie's last name was given as Trassjonsky on the charge sheet. Her solicitor's version later on was Trechjanskaya.

as "a curious brown corduroy jersey" with a blue skirt and a slouch hat of grey tweed, Trassjonsky a black jacket and striped skirt with a black velvet toque. Sir Homewood asked the presiding magistrate, Alderman Sir William Treloar, for a remand until the DPP could be represented. One witness, Inspector Thompson, was called.

Agitated but self-possessed, the two Jewesses sat huddled together in the narrow dock. They listened stiff-faced as the white-bearded interpreter, Aaron Lichtenstein, translated into Yiddish for them, nodding but otherwise showing little interest. They preferred to say nothing at present, Lichtenstein reported. Treloar having adjourned until 29th December, the prisoners were removed to Holloway Prison.

8. A Public Funeral

Two men who probably knew as much as anyone about the couple who first occupied 11 Exchange Buildings were James Curran and George More, who worked for the gas contractor and had spent several hours in their company on Saturday and Monday, 3rd and 5th December. From Curran's description of him and other details, the man must have been Joe Levi (alias Max Smoller), who originally rented no. 11 and had moved in a day or two before. He was about 5 feet 8 inches tall, Curran told the *Evening News*, and clean-shaven, with dark, curly hair, dark eyes and a sallow complexion. His manner was "affable", and he spoke English fluently. The woman (no doubt his wife) was "exceptionally finely built, so well built that I passed a remark to my mate about it".

Curran was positive both were Jews. According to him, two of the Grove Street set of six chairs were in the parlour and two in the first-floor bedroom; the third was probably taken downstairs later on as more people began to frequent the tenement. Levi was difficult about providing enough light to work by; on Saturday he eventually removed two of the three shutters, but on Monday he refused to take down more than one. His wife had not had time to put up curtains, he explained. He tipped the two men 8d, saying "Here's a glass of ale for you." The contractor's carman, who also called at no. 11 on 3rd December, collected a scrawled signature that looked like 'Mr Leve'.

The police had high hopes of Curran and More and called them over to Bishopsgate Street to see if their shapely young woman could conceivably be one of the two held. The confrontation proved abortive. "We had no difficulty," More commented, "in saying that there was no woman like her in the dozen we were shown."

With the memorial service and public funeral due the next day, wreaths and floral tributes flooded into the City mortuary on Wednesday. Amongst the senders were other police forces all over the country and the dead men's comrades of C Division, whose remembrance was a broken column of flowers; three paper-sellers on Finsbury Pavement; the Union of Street Hawkers and the London Cab-Drivers' Trade Union. A small bunch of lilies was received on behalf of Mrs Bentley, whose baby—a boy—was born on Wednesday morning. From "the Jewish Quarter of Houndsditch" came a gateway of white flowers and evergreens bearing the words 'The Gates of Heaven'; the message read "To the memory of the dear heroes who lost their lives in trying to defend their fellow creatures. God rest their souls." Harris the jeweller's tribute bore the single word 'Duty'. Six open landaus had to be added to the funeral procession, two preceding each hearse, to accommodate all the flowers.

A memorial service at St Paul's for three City policemen of low rank created many precedents. More than three thousand seats in the outer nave, not required for special mourners, were taken up fully half an hour before the noon service; the great cathedral was full to the doors, and at least ten thousand people awaited the procession in the churchyard. The prevailing mood was sombre, even the gutter tradesmen dispensing their memorial cards in an undertone. Churchyard vantage-points were occupied by ten o'clock, and halfway down Ludgate Hill men scrambled on to the roofs of vehicles for a better view.

Flags in the City fluttered at half-mast; many windows showed drawn blinds or mourning-boards. Many businesses closed. All Stock Exchange transactions were halted for an hour, enabling hundreds of clerks to watch the subsequent funeral procession to Ilford pass along Threadneedle Street. Weepers[1] were in evidence everywhere; horse-bus drivers had black crape tied to their whips. To enable the City Police to attend in strength, the streets of the City were kept by their Metropolitan *confrères*; all the policemen on this special duty, as well as those at St Paul's, wore black gloves.

The occasion fully maintained the period's exacting standards of ceremonial and controlled emotionalism. King George V was represented by his Groom in Waiting, Edward Wallington, and the Home Office by the Secretary of State, Winston Churchill, and Permanent Under-Secretary, Sir Edward Troup; many uniformed official bodies participated, and splendidly robed City dignitaries were present in full force. The procession reached the steps of the Cathedral at precisely twelve o'clock, whereupon the hundreds of special mourners took their seats, and colleagues of the dead men bore their coffins, upon each of which lay the helmet, belt and truncheon of its occupant, through the West Door. Here the coffins were met by ninety-one-year-old Dean Gregory and the choir and conducted to three purple-draped catafalques standing before the chancel gates.

After the service, in a pregnant silence broken sporadically by muted commands, the clatter of hooves and the jingle of harness, the *cortège* re-formed and moved off. As the procession passed Houndsditch on its way along Bishopsgate Street, the bands, which had been silent, broke again into Chopin's Funeral March. When the City boundary in Aldgate was reached, Choat's coffin departed for Waterloo Station whilst those of Bentley and Tucker, escorted by mounted City constables, set out for the cemetery.

During the 8-mile journey, made before an estimated 750,000 onlookers, flowers were frequently thrown from windows. The

---

[1] Generally hat-sashes for men and veils for women, both of black crape.

East End crowds watched in silence; their sympathy was manifest.[2] The sun shone fitfully during the brief afternoon, finally sinking behind a huge dun-coloured cloud. Of the many descriptions of the two sergeants' committal, this paragraph from the *News of the World* is perhaps as evocative as any:

> The light was failing when at last the carriages entered the burial-grounds, and a more sombre and stately ending to a great tribute could not have been devised. There were the heavy stone portals of the last place of all, the shadows of the poplars in the mist out of which the still day was dying, and Beethoven's Funeral March. Round the graves, which were made side by side on the south side of the grounds, the dim crowds gathered. There was the voice of the clergyman over the rites (a baby was crying in its mother's arms), and the two comrades were committed to the dust. One could hear the women in tears. But worse than the weeping of the women was the broken singing of the men, after the coffins were lowered, "When our heads are bowed with woe".

Choat's body lay overnight in Juniper Cottage, the family's Byfleet home, and was interred in the family grave on Friday. Every house and shop in the village had its blinds drawn. Both parents being dead, the constable's chief mourners were his four brothers and sisters. Detachments of the City, Metropolitan and Surrey police were present. Four additional carriages carried wreaths and floral tributes; there were more than 150. Choat too was committed as the last feeble rays of sunlight left the sky.

At about 2 p.m. on Thursday, 22nd December, two days after the *Evening News* had published an interview with Yourka Duboff, Detective Inspector Newell of the City Police called on him at his lodgings in Shepherd's Bush. Newell had brought no interpreter, but Duboff's landlady, a strongly maternal German *hausfrau* called Elsa Petter, came to his rescue periodically with translations. Her lodger made a short statement in pidgin English. He began by denying all knowledge of 59 Grove Street

---

[2] But there seems to have been at least one exception. A young Russian who claimed to know him well told the *Daily Chronicle* later that he had been walking along Osborn Street (a turning out of the Whitechapel Road) towards the route of the procession when he was amazed to see a short, blond man with square, bent-forward shoulders pacing up and down the pavement waiting for it. He was alone and dressed exactly as usual, and he seemed quite unperturbed.

and its lodgers, as he had to the *News*. The police knew he was acquainted with Peter the Painter, the inspector pointed out; he would be well advised to come to Old Jewry and make a full statement. The policemen searched the house but found nothing incriminating. Much upset, the young Lett became truculent. "You make mistake, terrible, gross," he declared vehemently as he left.

No interpretation at all was provided when Duboff made his second statement, also to Newell and also in broken English. The substance of this has already been given. It included an alibi for the time of the murders which Mrs Petter was able to corroborate. He had gone straight back from Grove Street to Shepherd's Bush, Duboff said, and had not left 20 Galloway Road again that night. He admitted also knowing Fritz. He visited the East End to buy Russian cigarettes and once had chanced to see a handbill for a balalaika concert at the Jubilee Street club. He described meeting Peter the Painter for the first time there, when they discovered they were both painters. Peter told him he had a £30 job for a shipping company.

That same afternoon, acting on information received, the police also visited 48 Turner Street, a thoroughfare connecting the Whitechapel Road with the Commercial Road. In the ground-floor front room were found photographs of several Eastern European men, letters addressed in various names, revolutionist literature and a Lettish Social Democratic Party membership card. Detective Inspectors Wensley and Collinson (of the City Police) were waiting in the room when, at about 8.30 p.m., its occupier walked in.

This was Jacob Peters, first cousin of Fritz Svaars. Peters was another young Lett, high-cheekboned, heavy-browed and amply endowed with the thick, disorderly head of hair so common amongst his compatriots; he was also stockily built, with a muddy complexion and a prominent broken nose. His seedy working-clothes did nothing to improve an unprepossessing appearance.

Peters showed no ill feeling and offered information quite freely. Told first of all that the police were inquiring into the Exchange Buildings murders, he replied "I don't care. I know nothing at all about it. I can't help what my cousin Fritz has done." Other remarks he made were, "I think that one of the men who has done that work is my cousin Fritz because in his room a dead man was found," and "We disagree with Fritz in many ways. He is an Anarchist, but, although I am a revolutionary, I am a Social Democrat." He had visited 59 Grove Street two or three times during the past few weeks, he said, but not before. Besides being secretary of the London branch of the Lettish Social Democratic Party, Peters belonged to the English Social Democratic Party and the Working Men's Federated Union; he handed over membership cards of these and also claimed an alibi: "I expected this every day. In case the police want to know what happened that night, they may call my landlady's attention to the fact that on that particular evening I was engaged in setting a mouse-trap. When I left work, I went to a provision shop facing Turner Street, bought some food there, took it home and never went out again. I went to bed about twelve o'clock." He had no fear and only wanted to tell the truth, Peters said when cautioned on arrival at Old Jewry. He then made a formal statement to Inspector Collinson through Russian interpreter Casimir Pilenas.

Peters's relationship to Fritz Svaars and revolutionary connections perhaps compensated for his absence from the Grove Street gathering of 16th December. Of those men who had been present, the police had ceased to detain one, Tocmacoff, and detained another, Duboff; and at 11 p.m. on Thursday they detained the only other participant who was known about, was still at liberty and had not disappeared—Josef (or Osip) Fedoroff.

Fedoroff, who lodged at 141 Romford Street, another of the many mean streets lying between the Whitechapel and Commercial Roads, was visited by Wensley and Detective Sergeant Richardson. As they climbed the stairs to Fedoroff's room, wondering what sort of reception was in store for them, the gas suddenly faded, and the whole house was plunged into darkness. Nothing else happened, however, and light was soon restored. The two detectives had brought no interpreter, and Fedoroff relied on his landlord's free translation of some of their questions. Had he been at the Grove Street gathering? Fedoroff nodded his bushy head immediately; yes, he had. Requested to go to City Police headquarters and give a full account of himself, he replied "Very well. I wasn't there when they did it."

At Old Jewry Fedoroff made a long statement through Pilenas. Much of this has already been recorded. His parents were dead; his brother was a police constable in Russia; he had arrived in England on this, his second visit, about 3½ months before. He was willing to answer all questions put to him. He thought he knew Peter (the Painter) but could not say anything about him. He said he did not recognize Gardstein's photograph.

Fedoroff also described Fritz's endeavours to find him employment. One at least of these hardly demonstrated the influence which the theatrical young Lett liked others to believe he possessed. On 12th December Fritz had taken Fedoroff to a factory off the City Road where, he said, he had once worked himself. He sent Fedoroff in while he waited outside. Fedoroff had a word with the 'guv'nor' in a corridor and was not given a job.

Although these three suspects were now held pending further inquiries, it was of course significant that none of them had changed his address after the murders, had had a firearm in his possession or offered the smallest resistance on being detained. This was hardly consistent with their being important characters in the main drama.

Newspaper accounts of the search for the major characters were meanwhile obliged to devote more and more space to incidentals and less and less to tangible progress. Despite the death of one of the villains, despite Rosie Trassjonsky's detention and the surrender of Luba Milstein, despite six days of London's biggest hue-and-cry since the 'Jack the Ripper' murders in 1888, the wanted men remained as elusive as ever.

A fundamental difficulty lay in obtaining reliable descriptions of them; these, vital to any real progress, often varied in basic detail from one informant to another. The conviction was general that the fugitives were being sheltered by compatriots who, from either sympathy or fear of reprisal, were keeping silent.

The small City force[3] was experiencing an additional

[3] The total establishments of the two forces on 29th September 1910 were: Metropolitan, 17,400; City, 1,181. The Metropolitan establishment permitted the

vexation—having to receive second-hand from the Metropolitan Police much information from the public about its own case. On their return from Ilford on Thursday, senior City officers joined their Metropolitan collaborators in a further conference. Nott-Bower then announced that he had been authorized to offer a reward of £500. Great confidence was felt that this would soon retrieve the situation.

9. Three Bewildered Prisoners

On Friday evening, 23rd December, a series of identification-parades was held in the muster room at Bishopsgate Street. Isaac Levy, who had already identified Gardstein as the man he had seen being assisted away from Exchange Buildings, now obliged further by identifying Peters and Duboff as the two men who had assisted him; and all three suspects were identified as having been seen in and around the cul-de-sac at various times.

An elementary irregularity was permitted, however. Although all the witnesses were looking for foreigners, only four or five of the men in the line-ups—including Fedoroff, Peters and Duboff—were not British. The subsequent police explanation, that they had tried to fill the line with men resembling foreigners, cut little ice when the multitude of genuine ones in the immediate vicinity was considered. If the officer in charge of the parades was Detective Chief Inspector Willis, as seems to have been the case, the lapse was a strange one for a policeman with thirty years' service.

At 9.30 on Saturday morning, Christmas Eve, the three men were charged with being concerned with Gardstein and others not in custody in the murder of the three policemen, also with conspiring with Trassjonsky, Milstein, Gardstein and others to

same number of superintendents as the City's of inspectors—28. The figures for constables were: Metropolitan, 14,478; City, 1,029. (Blue Book 64, 1911.)

rob Harris's shop. "We deny all knowledge and we are not guilty," Fedoroff answered. Peters and Duboff made the same reply.

They were then taken to Guildhall, where a large crowd had assembled in pouring rain to watch their arrival. Treloar was again the presiding magistrate. At 11.15, the City Solicitor and the Treasury Solicitor (representing the DPP) having arrived, the accused were put up.

Stale from thirty-six hours' imprisonment and still in his working-clothes, Peters cut a poor figure in the dock. Press descriptions of him dwelt on his shabby dress and physical limitations—the gilt stud at the neck of his collarless woollen shirt, his well worn dark-grey overcoat, his insignificant stature, low forehead, sunken eyes, broken nose and the rest. With his nondescript clothes, penetrating eyes, unruly moustache and mop of hair, Fedoroff fared little better. Duboff, on the other hand, with his "clean and neat" look, open countenance, smart brown lounge-suit, high white linen collar and bright green tie drew favourable comment even from *The Times*. The *Daily Mail* considered that he could almost pass as an Englishman.

With the three exotic prisoners present, a hush fell on the crowded little court-room. Again seeking a remand on minimum evidence, Sir Homewood Crawford thought Superintendent Ottaway's would suffice, but Treloar wanted to hear Isaac Levy. As the tobacconist's manager had not arrived, Fedoroff's detention was dealt with. Fedoroff explained through Russian interpreter Casimir Pilenas that he had understood little of what the police said when they called on him.

Anticipation ran high as Isaac Levy, a thickset, middle-aged figure in heavy overcoat and muffler, was sworn 'covered' in the Jewish fashion. His dark eyes roved nervously as he prepared to answer the City Solicitor's questions. His identification of Gardstein, Peters and Duboff was soon on record. Gardstein had seemed "dazed". The other two had pointed revolvers at him; speaking in broken English, one said "Don't follow us" and the other "Don't follow". He did not know which man said which.

"What did you do?"—"I ran away." (Laughter and "Silence!")

Up to this point Fedoroff (whose English was best) had shown more emotion than his two companions. The latter's composure disappeared abruptly when Pilenas gravely translated Levy's story to them; gesticulating violently, the two Letts strongly denied being the men referred to.

Sir Homewood called no further evidence, and, bewildered and frustrated, the three men were removed to Brixton Prison.

The first reward handbills, some in English and some in Yiddish, were issued from Old Jewry during Friday evening. They featured the police photograph of the dead man above the remark "Name said to be George Gardstein, alias Poolka Milowitz. Both may be incorrect" and a short description. Three persons were shown as wanted, Fritz Svaars (whose surname the police thus published for the first time), Peter the Painter and the woman in the three-quarter jacket and skirt. Their descriptions differed little from those already published. Both men, stated the new hue-and-cry unequivocally, were Anarchists; Fritz was a locksmith and a native of Libau. The £500 was payable in full for information leading to the arrest of all three or *pro rata*. The bills commanded close attention east of Aldgate Pump.

The belief that British criminals just did not shoot at policemen was widely held. On 27th December a labourer called Charles Arthur appeared before A. Chichele Plowden, a London magistrate, charged with attempting to murder a Metropolitan constable. The following exchange occurred between magistrate and accused:

Mr Plowden: "Is he an Englishman?"
Prisoner: "Yes, I am."
Mr Plowden: "I am sorry to hear it."
The *Daily Telegraph* could not swallow this. "The arrested man described himself as an Englishman," it reported, "but his appearance led observers to doubt this statement." Shortly, Arthur was said to have told the police, things would be different: "Mr Churchill is going to alter things, and we shall have a better chance, instead of being worried by you people." This led the *Telegraph* to publish a scathing leader in which Winston Churchill and Lloyd George (the Chancellor of the Exchequer) were called "the favourite statesmen of the criminal classes".[1]

[1] Insinuations that some kind of unholy alliance existed between the Radicals and

There was in fact disturbing evidence that events in Exchange Buildings had impressed a number of men who, like Charles Arthur, saw policemen as their natural enemies. A Derbyshire poacher threatened to ''do the Houndsditch affair'' on a police inspector; as a constable arrested three drunken men at Edmonton Green, an onlooker yelled ''Shoot him, shoot him, give him Houndsditch!''

The Jews continued to attract verbal slings and arrows. With a singular sense of timing, *The People* published on Christmas Day six verses of emotive doggerel called 'The Lessons of Houndsditch'. The composition was by a Madge St Maury, and its fifth verse ran:

> But I think it's time to plead once more
> > to get rid of the cursed breed
> Of alien Jews who seem to have been
> > the authors of the deed.
> Remember Tottenham! Foreign Jews
> > were the coward murderers there,
> And it's pretty certain that aliens held
> > the guns on the Houndsditch stair.

On this occasion, however, anti-Semitism had overreached itself. The St Maury diatribe brought a flood of letters of protest, many from Gentiles.

'Gardstein' was a Jewish name, but the superintendent of the Jews' Temporary Shelter, whose officials met every immigrant ship berthing in London, pointed out that Gentile criminals in Russia often resembled Jews in appearance, could speak Yiddish and assumed Jewish names. This served to put the police off the scent and sometimes even led them to organize a pogrom.

Jewish aliens in London did not lack Gentile champions. The Archbishop of York knew of no ''steadier, better conducted or more hard-working race of people'', he averred. The *Daily Express* recalled sociologist Charles Booth's remark that the children of Israel were East London's most law-abiding inhabitants.

Britain's lawbreakers were not uncommon at this time. On 25th June 1913 *Truth* remarked of Lord Robert Cecil: ''The Member for Hitchin has a certain definite faith which sustains him amid all adversity. It is that Radicals constitute the criminal class and that the only question is how many of them can be found out.''

This was the hey-day of the small private philanthropist in Britain, and if many saw the Exchange Buildings affair as a cudgel, many also saw it as an offertory plate. An *Express* fund for the victims' dependents did so well that it was closed after only four days. Contributors ranged from N. M. Rothschild & Sons, 100 guineas, to "May He give you your heart's desire", 2 shillings; Harris and his son sent 20 guineas each. Announcing the fund's closure at £1,813.9s.6d, the paper took a sharp dig at the City of London: "As the City Corporation, slow though it may be in coming to the determination to do something for its servants, will doubtless make some sort of provision by way of pensions for the widows, we think the additional sums subscribed by our readers are sufficient to place them all beyond possible want throughout life."

Feeling for Mrs Bentley and her new-born son was especially strong, and she was inundated with tokens of sympathy. The King sent his personal condolences through Nott-Bower. Lady Curzon Wyllie, whose husband had been assassinated in her presence eighteen months before, wrote saying that she well knew the sorrows such a tragic bereavement brought.

All City Police Christmas festivities had been abandoned and all leave for the force's hundred-odd detectives cancelled. Not one was at home for his Christmas dinner. Marathon spells of duty remained commonplace; food was snatched or gone without. With the holiday freedom of London's other citizens and the substantial reward on offer, hundreds of hours were spent investigating alleged suspicious characters. The uniformed branch also had its troubles: the two Bank Holidays which followed Christmas Day brought thousands of sightseers into the Exchange Buildings neighbourhood.

10. The Exemplary Lodger

The shock of recognition felt by Jacob Kempler when, walking in Mile End late on Tuesday afternoon, 27th December, he glanced at one of the reward handbills can be readily imagined. To Kempler, a Jewish bootmaker's foreman from Austria who now lived with his wife, Polly, and their four children at 44 Gold Street, the haughty, guarded eyes in the otherwise expressionless face were unmistakable. The notorious dead man of 59 Grove Street was none other than his absent lodger.

Gold Street, a short, unremarkable opening out of Stepney Green near the Mile End Road, lay about 1½ miles east of Houndsditch. It contained some tiny, ivy-covered cottages of the district's earlier rustic period but mostly the standard East End artisan dwellings, of which no. 44, with its weather-worn, blistered paint and threadbare curtains, was one. At about 7 p.m. two little girls and a crippled boy in the road watched "five Englishmen"—Chief Inspector Willis, Inspector Wensley and three H Division sergeants—jump out of their taxi-cab and gather round the front door.

An anxious and deferential Kempler admitted them. Giving evidence later, Willis defined one of their first discoveries in the congested rear ground-floor room as "like a student's outfit". This was a collection of bottles, nearly all medicine-sized, containing small quantities of chemicals and drugs. Amongst the former were diluted sulphuric acid, diluted nitric acid, caustic potash, mercury, carbon sulphide and phosphorus. With these things were a porcelain basin, a retort, tubes and scales. There were also several mechanical appliances, presumably for use in attacking safes. A brown leather portmanteau yielded up a dagger and a Belgian Browning automatic. In a cupboard and elsewhere were a belt containing 150 ·30 Mauser pistol cartridges gathered into clips of ten, 158 loose ·30 Mauser pistol cartridges and twenty-six Mauser rifle cartridges of another calibre. There was also an appliance that could be fitted to a Mauser pistol for firing from the shoulder.[1]

Another significant find was a mass of correspondence and printed matter, most of it in Russian and German but some in English. Amongst this were many revolutionist books, periodicals and pamphlets; one illustrated German volume dealt with "the melting and cutting of metals by means of acid and oxygen" and showed a blowpipe in use; another described various simple ways of manufacturing explosives.[2] There was also a trade-list of blowpipes available from a City Road firm. Some days later, when the correspondence had been translated, hares were to be started in St Petersburg, Moscow, Berlin, Vienna and elsewhere, not to mention a few in London. An expropriators' rendezvous in Paris was also disclosed. Other discoveries included photographs and two false passports, one of them in the name of John Stenzel. It was established that the dead man had been formally known as Poloski Morountzeff and that his preoccupation with larceny had arisen, at least in part, from his extreme Anarchist convictions.

The confusion of identities which plagued the Exchange Buildings affair continued. A signwriter called Abraham Morris had been the tenant of 44 Gold Street until 20th March 1910, when Kempler took over the house and Morris left on a visit to the United States. Morountzeff had engaged his 4-shilling-a-week room towards the end of Morris's tenancy, bore a superficial resemblance to him and up to 20th March had been seen only rarely. He also received letters in the name of Morin and was otherwise known to the Kemplers as Morintz. Thus almost all the lengthy random recollections which the neighbours provided for the popular newspapers were not of him but of Morris.

The Kemplers and Mr and Mrs Morris were dumbfounded at the news of their lodger's activities. Both couples had found him

---

[1] Usually designed for secondary use as a holster and sold with the pistol, the shoulder-stock to all intents and purposes converted it into a carbine.

[2] The revolutionary movement in Eastern Europe was so solidly established by this time that text-books for saboteurs and expropriators were in wide circulation.

quiet, unobtrusive and well behaved. He normally left his room in the afternoon—the Anarchist Club was only five minutes away—and returned about midnight. He described himself as a student of chemistry and attributed his leisurely existence and unusual affluence to remittances from wealthy parents.

His room, entered daily by his landlady to make the bed and tend the fire, was never seen to contain any indication of criminal habits. Once or twice, some weeks before the Exchange Buildings murders, Kempler had caught sight of the bottles. One day the bootmaker's curiosity overcame the diffidence his lodger's manner always inspired in him. "What bottles have you got there?" he inquired. Morountzeff explained, apparently off-handedly, that he was trying to formulate a fire-proofing paint.

At intervals Morountzeff would go away, sometimes for several weeks, and his room would be locked. He received occasional male visitors, other Eastern Europeans, but nobody knew much about them, with one exception—a tall, dark man called Josef. This man (undoubtedly Josef Sokoloff) was a frequent caller, and once, when Morountzeff was away, he brought Kempler a letter from 'Mr Morin' saying he could live in the room in his absence. Kempler permitted this for a time.

At 9 a.m. on Friday, 16th December, Polly Kempler's lodger came into her kitchen to wash his hands. "Mrs Kempler," he said, "I am going to leave London for the Continent. Will you lock my room and keep the things as they are for me?" The next time she saw him was in the mortuary. Josef was believed to have been his only caller during that last week. Neither he nor any of the dead man's other visitors had been seen since, and Kempler was later to testify that he could not identify any of them at Guildhall magistrates' court.

An early visitor to the Stepney bomb-factory, as it came to be called, was a small, clean-shaven, bustling man with cold, alert eyes; this was the DPP, Sir Charles Mathews, who also visited Grove Street and Exchange Buildings. Another caller at no. 44 was Superintendent Quinn. Gold Street became for a time a Mecca almost comparable with Exchange Buildings and 119 Houndsditch. Since 16th December hundreds of letters had poured into the little jeweller's shop. Country visitors to Town were particularly drawn to it; the Harrises soon grew accustomed to inquiries for trinkets required as souvenirs, and to the avid faces peering through the dusty window. One man from Norfolk left the shop in triumph with a Harris business-card which the good-natured proprietor had endorsed "Jock has been here" and signed.

To the average Briton of this period an Anarchist was a fanatical assassin of monarchs, senior statesmen and chiefs of police; he was also, needless to say, foreign. That he could specialize in robbery to swell the movement's funds (not to speak of his own) occurred to few people. If he was an active Anarchist, he of course threw bombs, and, perhaps naturally, Fleet Street's first theory was that Morountzeff and his accomplices had been manufacturing them. No home-made explosives of any sort had been found at 44 Gold Street, however, and no signs whatever of any attempt to make any. As the days went by, the fact that robbery rather than revolution had been the aim gradually sank in, and the Press moderated its alarm. Whether Morountzeff was an Anarchist or not, a senior Metropolitan Police officer remarked to the *Daily Telegraph*, had yet to be proved; all that seemed absolutely certain was that he was the 'brain' of an organization in Britain devoted to robbery. Forty-eight hours later a City Police spokesman told the *Daily Mail*: "The men who are being sought for, although doubtless Anarchists, are not in any way typical of that body. The ordinary Anarchist in this country is a law-abiding person. . . . No true Anarchist would shelter these men for a moment. Unfortunately, there are others of the same class as themselves, who rob and murder under the guise of Anarchism."

What further information did Scotland Yard require before it could concede that Morountzeff was an Anarchist? What kind of strange, two-headed animal was a law-abiding one? How did men who were "doubtless Anarchists" come to be acting lawlessly "under the guise of Anarchism"? Scotland Yard was determined to show that the Special Branch had not been caught napping, and Old Jewry hoped that shocked so-called Anarchists of the passive, theorizing variety might be cajoled into revealing the wanted men's whereabouts.

Although running them to earth was obviously of first importance at this point, public interest in their political status was intense. The *Daily Express* of Friday, 30th December, carried the following 'scoop':

> . . . the group of Anarchists of which the dead assassin Morountzeff was the leader in London . . . are revolutionaries of the most violent type. They are known as the 'Lettish Anarchist Communist Group, Leesa, London'. This title was printed in the form of a disc on letters which were found in the room of the dead man at the house in Gold Street.
>
> The London group was governed by a committee of twenty, of whom Morountzeff was the head. Their password used among themselves and at all their meetings was *'Brehoiba'*, the Lettish for 'Freedom'.
>
> The group was first formed in London in 1906, when a large number of Letts emigrated to England after the great strikes at Riga. Simultaneously, centres were formed throughout Europe, and the total number of members sworn to obey the commands of the leaders is now estimated at twenty thousand.
>
> The headquarters of the movement is at Hamburg and the supreme leader is one S—. Other centres are in New York, Berlin, Paris, St Petersburg and Vienna. . . .
>
> The committee was known as the Expropriation Committee. . . .
>
> Morountzeff was a man of desperate bravery and a clever chemist. He was one of the chief organizers in the whole movement and at intervals paid visits to different centres, his last journey being to Berlin some few weeks ago.

Meanwhile the police had traced the suppliers of the 40-cubic-foot cylinder of oxygen found at 9 Exchange Buildings. On 2nd December this firm had sold the pressure-gauge, a 6-cubic-foot cylinder of oxygen and various accessories including a pair of blue goggles to Enrico Malatesta, an Italian who had a small electrical and general engineers' business in the City Road. Ten days later Malatesta exchanged the smaller cylinder for the brand new 40-cubic-foot one, and four days after that—on the day of the murders—he returned the larger cylinder for recharging. This was done at once, and the cylinder was redelivered to his workshop at 15 Duncan Terrace, Islington.

This development brought the detectives firmly back to Anarchism. Now nearly sixty years old, Malatesta was a fiery, fanatical anti-authoritarian. His capacity for fomenting disorder had so provoked the Italian police that he was banished without trial to a small Mediterranean island; four years later, at the turn of the century, he escaped to political asylum in England. Enrico Malatesta was no low-born immigrant revolutionary but an Italian count who was said to have renounced his title and estates for the cause; more than this, his reputation as an Anarchist was international, and he was a man of influence, being a close friend of Prince Kropotkin and Prince Varlan Tscherkesoff and an acquaintance of Ramsay MacDonald, leader of the Labour Party (which had forty-two members in the newly elected House of Commons).[3] It was realized that this prickly Italian nobleman must be handled with great care.

Malatesta's story was predictably unhelpful. He had allowed Morountzeff, free of charge, the run of his workshop, which was equipped with tools for working metals of all kinds; during December Malatesta himself had been trying to make cycle-frames using a blowpipe with oxygen and coal-gas for brazing. He found the 40-cubic-foot cylinder unsatisfactory. On 15th December he was visited by a casual acquaintance called Lambert who said he needed oxygen for a 'limelight show' and purchased it, the pressure-gauge and a length of india-rubber tubing for £5. He put down £1 as a deposit. Before the cylinder was removed, the Italian had it recharged. He had not set eyes on Lambert since, he declared; and the police could not find him.

It was common for revolutionaries using several names outside the movement to have none at all inside it. He had known neither Morountzeff's name nor his address, Malatesta said, and had always referred to him simply as 'the Russian'. "There are plenty of police spies," he remarked later at Guildhall, "and one prefers not to know anything." They had met at the club in Jubilee Street.

Although Morountzeff had used his small workshop on and off for about nine months, Malatesta was vague about the other man's activities in it. He had seen him make "a kind of pump and small pieces of machinery". On 16th December Morountzeff was,

[3] Their acquaintanceship was acknowledged by MacDonald in a speech to the House of Commons on 22nd May 1912 and at other times. Prince Varlan Tscherkesoff, another aristocratic Russian Anarchist, was in turn a close friend of Leo Tolstoy.

as usual, working on some metals; when the Italian last saw him, late in the afternoon, he was adjusting two pieces of tubing. Malatesta identified much of the equipment found in Exchange Buildings but denied ever having seen the crowbars, drills and some other items before. Almost 4 feet long and weighing 56 pounds, the oxygen cylinder had been wrapped in brown paper, put into a specially made deal box and taken from Duncan Terrace to Exchange Buildings—a journey of about 1½ miles— during the afternoon of 16th December. A youth, seemingly English, paid Malatesta the £4 balance, removed the purchases on a costermonger's barrow and was later seen taking a long box and a bale into 9 Exchange Buildings. No one knew this lad, and nothing more was heard of him.

The City Police had sent particulars of Morountzeff and the five accused to various Continental forces with a request for information. As regards finding the remaining suspects, however, the policy of leaving no stone unturned was proving woefully insufficient. Amongst the East End's many thousand aliens must be two or three who knew the right stone to turn. If the search was not to drag on indefinitely, one of them would have to point it out.

11. Slow-Motion Law

More than sixty pressmen and artists attended the third Guild-hall sitting on Thursday, 29th December, and there was an undignified scramble even for standing-room. Security precautions were extremely strict. Treloar again presided, Nott-Bower attended, and present with the Treasury Solicitor to take up the DPP's case was the senior Treasury counsel, Archibald Bodkin.[1]

[1] Archibald Henry Bodkin had spent sixteen years as a junior Treasury counsel at the Central Criminal Court before receiving this appointment in 1908. He succeeded Sir Charles Mathews as DPP in 1920 and retired ten years later. The

All five accused were present and legally represented, Peters
and Fedoroff through the good offices of the Working Men's
Federated Union. The three men now appeared more composed.
They did not speak to one another, but the women whispered
and laughed softly during the long periods when only English
was to be heard; the more vivacious Trassjonsky, who glanced
round the courtroom from time to time with an inquiring smile,
set the example for their behaviour.

Bodkin, a spare, bald, beaky, word-spinning man whose dry
correctness would lapse occasionally and reveal an endearing
good nature, told the court that he did not expect to open the case
against the accused "for some little time"; nothing must be said or
done that might hamper police inquiries. Superintendent
Ottaway, whose unenviable task it was to direct those inquiries
and prepare the case for the DPP, listed his discoveries in
Exchange Buildings, and interpreter Pilenas then translated to
the prisoners, the exhibits being produced as they were mentioned. The three men's stolid demeanour vanished at once.
Duboff asked what the cylinder was for; Peters showed particular
curiosity about the combined wrench and cutter; Fedoroff knew
nothing about any of these implements, he announced; Milstein
turned a quill pen nervously in her fingers; Trassjonsky alone
remained bland and seemingly unconcerned.

Highly formalized and burdened with proprieties, English
judicial procedure is easily dislocated by exceptional circumstances. In particular, it is essential that the momentum of the
proceedings be maintained. The magisterial hearing was ill-fated
from the start in that so many factors combined to slow the pace
to a crawl: the hours occupied in translation, the number of
accused, the time spent treading water so as not to risk prejudic-
ing the police investigations, the brief and widely spaced initial
sittings and, above all, the extreme complexity of the case. By the
time it reached the Central Criminal Court, more than eighty

policy of the DPP in the early 1900s was still a harsh one, the determination to
obtain convictions commonly resulting in such unscrupulous tactics as the
suppression of evidence that favoured the accused; to Bodkin, a humane and
fair-minded man, belongs much of the credit for the slow but sure progress made
against this oppressive attitude during his twenty-two years as senior counsel
and Director.

witnesses had been called, the depositions took up 665 foolscap pages, and there were 141 exhibits.

The court adjourned until 6th January. Press coverage of the Exchange Buildings affair at the turn of the year was sparse. The New Year Honours included the five King's Police Medals; another went to Nott-Bower, who also received a knighthood. Bryant was now up and taking exercise; Woodhams's gradual improvement continued. The committee of Portsoken Ward, in which Exchange Buildings was situated, passed a resolution noting indignantly that the criminals were neither Jewish nor inhabitants of the Ward.

If the DPP felt an overriding solicitude for the police, and Fleet Street had been providing glowing daily accounts of their unremitting industry, less flattering opinions were also held. The *East London Observer*'s leader of 31st December was highly critical. Nobody could tell from the evidence permitted at the official inquiries whether they had not in fact bungled the job, it commented. Apparently the police could function properly only on information received; but for Morountzeff's death, they would still be hopelessly in the dark.

On Monday, 2nd January 1911, the police searchers certainly seemed to be deep in the doldrums. More interest was shown in the body found on Clapham Common early on New Year's Day and the old folk emerging from the workhouses to live on the newly introduced old-age pension of 5 shillings a week.

Police fortunes were about to improve, however. It had been established by now that the latest murder victim was Leon Beron and that he had lived in Jubilee Street, on H Division territory. Preoccupied with this new case, Inspector Wensley walked into Leman Street police-station at about midday on 2nd January to find a message from Old Jewry. Amongst the latest information received there about the Exchange Buildings case was an exceptionally promising item.

Wensley went to Old Jewry at once and talked with Chief Superintendent Stark and Superintendent Ottaway. Two young men, apparently Fritz Svaars and a friend known as Yoshka (the Russian version of Josef), were in touch with a woman in Stepney. City detectives expected to learn her name and address later in the day. The second man had a peculiar walk. Both men were understood to be armed and determined not to be taken alive. The three officers made contingency plans, and Wensley returned to Leman Street to await more news.

PART II

Retribution

12. Two Armed and Desperate Men

Wensley returned to Old Jewry at 6.30 p.m. for further discussions. The woman who was now supposed to be sheltering the pair had been identified to the police and been seen to enter a house in Sidney Street, a typically sombre Stepney thoroughfare running north-south from the Whitechapel Road across Oxford Street (since renamed Stepney Way) to the Commercial Road. The house was no. 100; almost opposite it, at no. 109, stood the small chemist's shop of Carl Cohen, in whose first-floor sitting-room a close watch was established. While the City Police placed great faith in their information, it was not certain that their quarry were in the house at that time.

At about midnight Superintendent Ottaway telephoned Wensley. All remained quiet around no. 100. The two men agreed that the time had come to force the issue. Wensley reported the situation to his divisional superior, Superintendent Mulvaney, and set out for the Metropolitan police station in Arbour Square, about ½ mile south-east of where no. 100 stood in upper Sidney Street.

The three superintendents joined a large body of detectives and uniformed men assembling in the little police-station, and, at about 12.30 a.m. on Tuesday, 3rd January, a conference took place on the vexed question of how to attempt the arrests. Assuming that, as the tip-off had suggested, the two men were in the house but might well leave it during the night, the general view was that it would be best to intercept them when they emerged into the street. Mulvaney wrote in his subsequent report to the Metropolitan Police Commissioner:

> We decided to establish a blockade of the house, 100 Sidney Street,
> where they were believed to be, rather than sacrifice valuable lives in
> attempting their capture by rushing the place, which . . . would also

have afforded opportunities of escape in the confusion. Consequently, two hundred men of the City and Metropolitan Police forces established cordons, and every avenue of escape from front or rear was guarded by armed police. Armed constables were also placed in the front room of 111 Sidney Street, which, with yard adjoining, is occupied by Mr Dickholtz, a carman, and which house is immediately opposite 100 Sidney Street. Armed constables were also placed in the doorways of houses where practicable in Sidney Street.[1]

About half this blockading force were City men.

The late hour and miserable weather helped the police to conceal their unusual activity; it was two o'clock before, in bitter cold with flurries of sleet and snow, the cordons around no. 100 were fully established.

Nos. 98–112 Sidney Street (even numbers only, ascending northwards) fronted on to the pavement along the east side of the street. Called Martin's Mansions after Charles Martin, their owner, the block was bounded by Lindley Street to the north and Hawkins Street to the south. Each of the eight houses, which had been built (in garish red Fletton brick) as recently as 1900, contained three main floors and a spacious attic within a mansard roof; the terrace effectively dwarfed the two-floored workmen's cottages and occasional dilapidated shops across the road from it. Behind each line of buildings lay a labyrinth of yards, sheds and passages. Immediately to the north-west of those on the west side of the street rose the great brewery of Mann, Crossman & Paulin with its bottling-department, cooling-tower and long yard at the southern end. The massive, gaunt building and taller tower in turn dominated Martin's Mansions, no. 100 standing only some 70 yards from their grimy walls.

By 3.30 it was clear that the wanted pair, whether aware of their danger or not, were most unlikely to make a move before daybreak. The men crouching in adjacent alleys, back yards and doorways had already settled down to a long vigil. "The poor Jewish population of the neighbourhood were kindness itself to us," Inspector Collinson told the *Daily Mail* afterwards,

---

[1] P.R.O./Metpol/5/110: *S.St.Fin—Compensation Claims*. Much of the background information about the siege contained in Parts II and III comes from this file.

"making us hot coffee and placing articles of furniture at our disposal."

The Metropolitan officers at least had still to be convinced that the two men were in the house; nor was anything known about the other occupants. The two City superintendents, Wensley and other officers established a base in no. 102, the home of a family called Blustein.

The occupants of the front ground-floor room of no. 100 were then roused. These proved to be a middle-aged master ladies' tailor named Samuel Fleischmann, his alert, loquacious wife Rebecca, their pretty seventeen-year-old daughter and their baby girl. Interpreter Harry Wagner's gentle but insistent tapping on the window woke both parents, who mistook him for the milkman. Drowsily, Samuel told his wife to tell him not to come so early; Rebecca got up and called through the window that she did not need any milk.

The tapping continued. He wanted to see Mr Fleischmann, Wagner told Rebecca. Samuel described what happened next to the Compensation Board which was subsequently set up:

> I . . . opened the window blind, and I saw a gentleman, a stout fellow, and I asked him "What is it?" and he said in Jewish "Don't be afraid; come out." I said "Who are you?" He said "I am from the police." I did not believe him; he was in private clothes. I said to my wife "You come out with me." I opened the street door, and he says to me "Be quiet; come out and everything will be safe."

Samuel was reassured by the sight of a police revolver and truncheon. He and his wife dressed hastily, Rebecca in jacket, skirt and boots. Chief Superintendent Stark began the interrogation directly they arrived, blinking, in the Blustein's brightly lit front room. The nimbler-witted Rebecca supplied most of the answers.

Her husband was the direct tenant of no. 100. They had three sub-tenants. The main part of the house contained a front and a back room on each of its first three floors, with a single attic room above; behind these were a kitchen on the ground floor and an additional room above it. The middle ground-floor room was occupied by a couple called Clements, the husband ninety-one years old and bedridden, his wife similarly advanced in years.

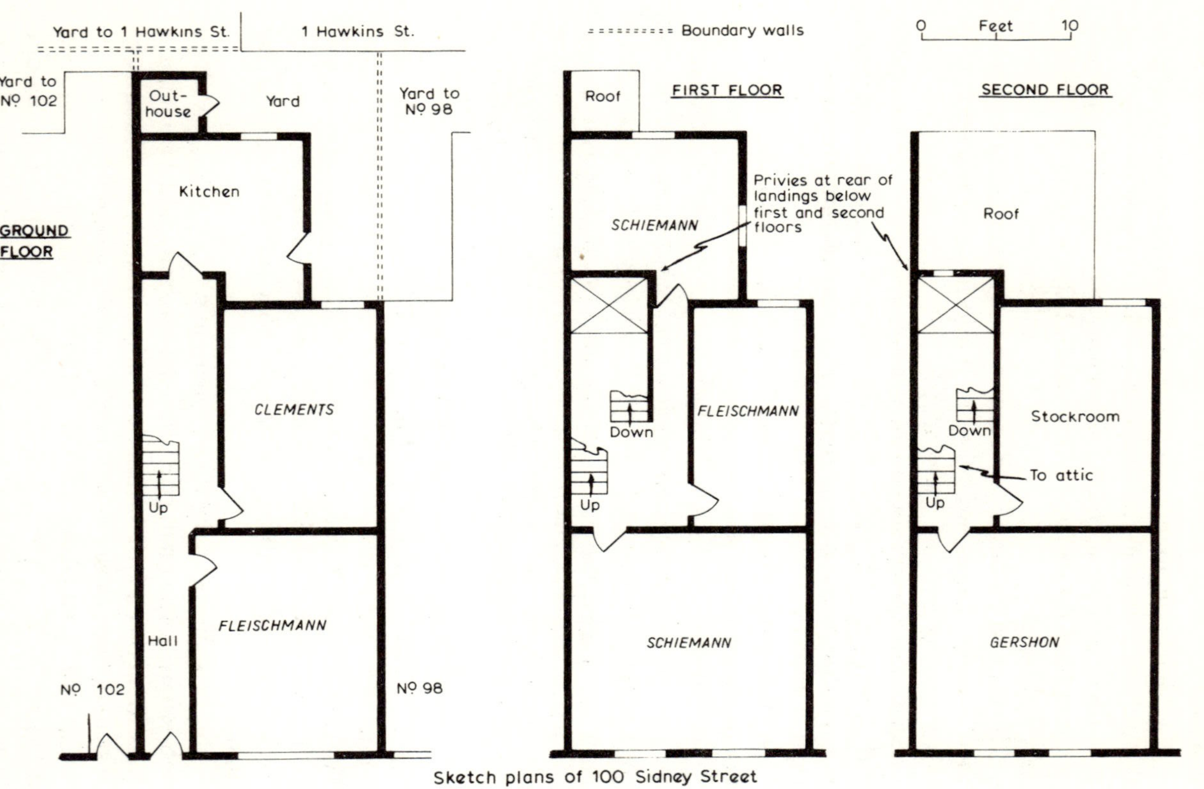

Sketch plans of 100 Sidney Street

Two of the three first-floor rooms, the front one and the one over the kitchen, were let to Davis Schiemann, a ladies' tailor from Russian Poland; Schiemann, his wife and their two infants shared the front room and their two older children the one at the back. The Fleischmanns' fourteen-year-old son and his younger brother slept in the middle first-floor room. No one occupied the rear second-floor room and attic, which served as stockroom and workroom respectively for the Fleischmann tailoring business. By herself in the second-floor front room lived Mrs Betsy Gershon, a Jewish dressmaker in her late twenties from the Crimea. The Fleischmanns had occupied the house since it was built; the Schiemanns had been with them nearly four years, the Clementses two years and Mrs Gershon eighteen months.

Rebecca was asked to describe Mrs Gershon and did so: tall, with longish nose and thin face. Did she wear spectacles? Yes, said Rebecca, folders. The officers exchanged glances.

Samuel's account went on:

> When I came in there, I saw so many officers in Mr Blustein's house—of course they gave me a chair, and my wife, to sit in, and they asked me to go upstairs and call Mrs Gershon down. Of course, seeing so many officers there, I think there must be something serious in my house and I say "No, I would not go for a thousand pounds." There was Mr Wensley there. . . .
>
> I did not know his name at the time; only, of course, I knew everybody there was an officer—I said to him "Why don't you go?" After they see they cannot do anything with me, they ask my wife to go up.

The likelihood that two armed and desperate men would be close at hand in the dark, silent house was not mentioned. The more biddable Rebecca dutifully complied. Wensley, on his own (H Division) territory and playing a characteristically dominant part in the proceedings, devised a cover story for her: Samuel had been ill during the summer; she could pretend he had been taken ill again and ask Mrs Gershon to fetch the doctor.[2]

---

[2] Rebecca later told the Compensation Board that, if she had "thought there was anybody up there", she would certainly not have gone. In that era police behaviour towards the 'lower orders' was often unfeeling to the point of brutality. Wensley was a dedicated policeman and, undoubtedly, a courageous man; he

An officer accompanied her to the front door of no. 100, immediately beside no. 102's, and stood about awaiting her return. Rebecca knew of no reason for being especially quiet, and he listened to the receding sound of her boots on the stairs above.

There was no light on the stairs or in the second-floor passage. Reaching the door of her lodger's room, Rebecca knocked twice and called out "Mrs Gershon, Mrs Gershon."

The room remained silent. At that moment the stockroom door on her left opened, and Betsy Gershon emerged. She was in her petticoat and had no boots on.

"What are you doing in the stockroom?" demanded Rebecca, her surprise tinged with disapproval.

The other woman answered without apparent hesitation. As both knew, the meter controlling her gas-supply was in this room. She felt queer, she said, and had been putting a penny into it to "make something for herself".

Rebecca seized this opening. Her husband too was feeling bad. Mrs Gershon could come downstairs, and she would give them both a drop of brandy. Mrs Gershon could then go and fetch the doctor.

Both women were also aware that Schiemann usually ran this errand when Samuel was ill. There was a pregnant pause.

"Ain't there nobody else?" Betsy asked.

"No, Mrs Gershon," said Rebecca firmly. "I think you will do."

On the lowest landing Betsy halted with an exclamation. The street door was open.

"Oh, don't look at that," said Rebecca, resourceful as ever. "I called someone in from the street."

Betsy then realized that Rebecca had passed her own room and was heading for the front door. "You are going the wrong way," she cried. The waiting officer rushed in, seized her and bore her into no. 102.

For a while Betsy tried sullenly to parry the police questions.

was also an exceptionally foxy one, and some of his stratagems showed his capacity for guile to better advantage than his moral sense. In his memoirs he wrote that when 59 Grove Street was raided on 17th December, believing that murderers might be lurking in the first-floor rooms, he compelled Lizzie Katz to precede him up the stairs. "Her bulk amply protected me from any possible bullet. . . ." Frederick Porter Wensley, *Detective Days* (Cassell, 1931), p. 158.

The Fleischmanns listened in horrified silence. Piece by piece, largely in English but occasionally in Yiddish, the essence of her story emerged. She had lived at 100 Sidney Street since her husband returned to Russia. On Sunday evening and again last evening a friend of theirs had visited her. This man, whom she knew only as Yoshka, was tall and dark and had an odd walk. Neither visit was expected, and Yoshka had been accompanied on both by another man who was short and fair. Betsy had never met him before and did not know his name; Yoshka had called him "pal".

On Sunday the two men spent about an hour and a half with her between eight and ten; on Monday they did not arrive until about 10.30 and showed no inclination to leave. Some time after midnight she asked them outright to do so. They refused. Betsy then threatened to raise her voice and call her landlady. They told her she must keep quiet, showed her their fists and, taking her skirt and boots to prevent her from going downstairs, turned her out of the room. She withdrew into the stockroom under their watchful eyes.

The position was now clear. Firstly, the fugitives were present and hardly likely to be taken unawares. Secondly, no. 100's stairs were straight, steep and only 2 feet 6 inches wide; the flights to the first and second floors included a 5 foot 3 inch landing giving a 180-degree turn three-quarters of the way up to each floor. Obliged by the narrow hall and stairs to advance in single file, an army of policemen could easily be wiped out from above by a determined defence with automatic pistols. If a bloodbath were to be avoided, the embargo on a rush must obviously remain. Thirdly, there were still a dozen men, women and children between the street door and the wanted pair.

In a forlorn hope, Betsy was sent back into no. 100 to see if she could persuade either of them to fetch the doctor. She returned saying that she could not. It was then decided that the remainder of the household must be evacuated.

With considerable help from Wagner, a philosophical man who remained unruffled, Rebecca bore the brunt of this operation also. Next to arrive in no. 102, excited curiosity vying with sleepiness, were the four Fleischmann children. The reactions of

Davis Schiemann and his wife, woken by Rebecca at four o'clock and told there were "two murderers upstairs", are not hard to imagine. To speed them on their way, Rebecca bustled off with one of their babies on each arm. The parents and their two older children, aged nine and eleven, soon followed. Mr and Mrs Clements, however, proved almost impossible to dislodge; the old man screamed with fear and protest, and at the height of the clamour someone blew a police whistle. Samuel went back to his house and into the Clements's room three times, trying to get the old man out.

Chief Inspector Willis, who apparently shared the widely felt impatience at the roundabout tactics adopted, entered and left no. 100 without delicacy; the sizeable police party in no. 102, however, largely dissociated itself from the evacuation.

Wearing a coat and boots borrowed from Rebecca, Betsy was removed to Arbour Square and then to Bishopsgate Street. No. 98, at the southern end of Martin's Mansions, was occupied by Dr Solomon Krestin; four armed policemen had been stationed in no. 98's yard, and another four in no. 102's, since before two o'clock. These two houses were not evacuated, but Isaac Dickholtz, the coal merchant and haulier directly opposite the blockaded house, sent his wife and children off to friends.

As the neighbourhood was densely populated and the situation seemed certain to attract large and possibly excitable crowds, reinforcements (a hundred men from each force) had been called for at about 4 a.m.

It was nearly five o'clock before Clements was carried bodily out of no. 100. The two fugitives had remained inactive throughout the evacuation but must have been aware of it. The street door stood open so that the hall and stairs could be watched, but after a while the gaslight began to grow dimmer; Inspector Collinson, Detective Sergeant Leeson and others hurried back in, located the ground-floor meter and put more pennies into it. At about 6.45, from across the street, Chief Superintendent Stark saw the door of the first-floor front room open and shut. Policemen in and around the front of the house were warned.

It was now considered that there was nothing more to be done until first light, due about three-quarters of an hour later.[3] From seven o'clock until the blockade ended, Yoshka and his companion had the house entirely to themselves.

13. A Shooting Match

Groups of early workers were by now collecting rapidly behind the outer cordons. The three superintendents and Wensley had crossed the road and established a new command-post in Dickholtz's yard, at the rear of which another consultation was held. Although the police could not start any shooting, the moment had come to press matters further. Completely surrounded and overwhelmingly outnumbered, the wanted men must be offered a formal opportunity to surrender.

Others in and near the yard at this time included Chief Inspector Willis and Inspectors Thompson, Collinson and Hallam of the City Police, also Detective Sergeants Leeson, Richardson, Boreham and Weston of H Division. The widespread sense of frustration continued to produce pleas for a rush and isolated acts of bravado; Stark later testified that an officer he did not know had marched up to the street door of no. 100 and thumped loudly on it. This brought no response.

The casual police attitude towards communication with suspected aliens in their own tongue evinced itself once more, and the simple expedient of employing an interpreter and a megaphone seems to have occurred to no one. Instead, a more provocative method of gaining the fugitives' attention was chosen: throwing pebbles up at the two windows of the second-floor front room they were presumed still to be in.

The superintendents watched this manoeuvre from the archway entrance to Dickholtz's yard. For a second or two it also

[3] On 3rd January 1911 sunrise was at 8.8 and sunset at 4.1.

seemed to have drawn a blank. Leeson, Richardson, Hallam, Collinson and others stood momentarily in the slush watching the closed, lace-curtained windows. Wensley turned back to find more pebbles. Suddenly a first-floor window-pane shattered as a stream of bullets poured through it, raking the group and the yard entrance and bouncing off the walls.

There was a headlong dive for cover. One bullet sang past Collinson's coat sleeve. Hallam was temporarily deafened by another which pierced the rim of his felt hat. Two almost simultaneous jolts, accompanied by a shocked numbness in his chest, told Leeson he was less fortunate.

Standing in another yard entrance nearby, Detective Inspector Hine of the City Police returned the fire. The fight was on.

Leeson stumbled towards Wensley and the archway, calling out "I am shot." Richardson supported him to the rear of the yard. Leeson and Wensley had started out together as constables in Whitechapel in the late 1880s and were brother Freemasons; the inspector came to him at once. "I am dying," the heavily built sergeant gasped. "They have shot me through the heart. Give my love to the children. Bury me at Putney." The two men embraced. "I am with you to the last," said Wensley. "I know that, Fred," Leeson answered.

The other bullet had injured his right foot. He was carried into the back room of no. 109. An onlooker, a coffee-stall keeper called Lewis Levy, at once volunteered to fetch a doctor. Setting off northwards across walls and fences, Levy brought back Dr Nelson Johnstone, assistant to a practitioner at 78 Mile End Road.[1] The doctor, half-dressed but fortunately in fair athletic shape, later told the *Daily Telegraph*:

> I was called about half-past seven o'clock by a man who said a policeman had been shot in Sidney Street. When I got there, I was taken into the brewery yard and had to climb over a gateway, up ladders and scramble over the roof of outbuildings to get to the place. Firing was going on the whole of the time. I found poor Leeson lying on a couch in the room. His shirt was open, and I saw a wound in the left breast. I found that the bullet had made its exit

[1] Going eastwards, the Whitechapel Road becomes the Mile End Road at the top of Sidney Street.

from the right breast, having gone across the body with a slight downward movement.

I attended to him, and he spoke about his wife and children and asked me if it was "all up with him". I said "No, you will be all right." We gave him some brandy, and he revived. He put his hand into his pocket and produced his revolver, saying "Here is my revolver, it is no more use to me." I put it in my hip pocket. The question then arose, how we were to get him to the hospital, for all the time the firing was going on. . . .

Only one route presented itself: over the 10-foot boundary wall at the back of Dickholtz's yard, across the roof of one of the out-houses behind it and down into the brewery yard. The shooting having brought the superintendents other urgent responsibilities, it fell to Wensley to oversee his injured colleague's removal.

Sergeant Boreham obtained a stretcher from the brewery, where a number of employees, including Frank Gascoyne, a Boer War veteran, came forward eagerly as helpers. Leeson was put into the stretcher, a cart drawn up against the wall and a ladder placed in it. By a combined effort the stretcher was coaxed up on to the outhouse roof. On the far side were two step-ladders for bringing the casualty down and more men waiting to accept him.

As the stretcher was gradually approaching its destination, however, a uniformed policeman climbed one of the step-ladders, and his helmet appeared above the wall.[2] Both wall and roof could be seen from the large attic window of 100 Sidney Street some 40 yards away. Although thick, swirling snow was falling, the party immediately found itself under rapid and well directed fire. Everyone not controlling the stretcher withdrew precipitately. "You are taking me into the line of fire again," observed Leeson with feeling. For the next ten minutes his bearers crouched and slithered in the soot, mud and half-melted snow while bullets whizzed around them; one narrowly missed the doctor's forehead, and a detective constable was hit on the hand. Eventually Leeson rolled himself off the stretcher, scrambled across the intervening space and was assisted down from the other side. At about 8.30, an hour after being shot, he was admitted to the London Hospital.

[2] Giving evidence later, Wensley was explicit that the culprit was a City man.

Having disposed of the stretcher and seen all the others out of danger, Wensley then found himself pinned down. Unlike his wounded sergeant, the inspector was slim and wiry. Noticing that the outhouse gutter was partly hidden from no. 100's view by the top of the wall, he found a miserable sanctuary there, lying doggo in an inch of muddy, half-frozen water. It did not occur to him until afterwards that he could have removed some tiles and lowered himself through the gap. Finally his distant assailant's attention was diverted, and he too regained safety.

Further police reinforcements were sent for when the shooting began, and by 9 a.m. about 750 men, some of them mounted, were on the scene. The crowds already numbered several thousands.

After firing their first volley, Yoshka and his friend lost no time demonstrating their fighting spirit and the superiority of their position and weapons. By comparison with their wide command of front and rear from no. 100's attic and second-floor windows, the besiegers everywhere were cramped and earthbound. The pair ranged the deserted house freely, sometimes firing simultaneously from different floors. They seem to have been too excited to take careful aim, but the occasional policeman, uniformed or otherwise, breaking cover outside was fortunate if bullets did not start dancing round him.

Nor in the early stages were the two men much concerned about more than their arms, hands and weapons being seen. One of several people who gained a clear sight of them was Sergeant Thurlow, in charge of about twenty City policemen immediately behind no. 100. Both attic windows were uncurtained; their faces were visible just above the sill of the back one. The "very dark man", as the sergeant later described him, had a pistol in each hand—both Mausers, he thought—and fired about six rounds into the backyards of nos. 98, 100 and 102. Thurlow, who had a heavy Adams revolver, loosed off three shots at the men. They disappeared at once.

He would have been astonished if he had hit one of them. The firearms supplied to the inner police cordons were few and unimpressive. Some Metropolitan men carried slow-firing, short-range revolvers of the old bulldog pattern. Thurlow and

THE ILLUSTRATED LONDON NEWS,

REGISTERED AT THE GENERAL POST OFFICE AS A NEWSPAPER.

3742.—VOL. CXXXVIII. | SATURDAY, JANUARY 7. 1911. | SIXPENCE.

The Copyright of all the Editorial Matter, both Engravings and Letterpress, is Strictly Reserved in Great Britain, the Colonies, Europe, and the United States of America.

ME SECRETARY AS DIRECTOR OF THE "BATTLE" OF THE EAST END: MR. WINSTON CHURCHILL DURING THE SIEGE OF THE HOUSE IN SIDNEY STREET. OFF THE MILE END ROAD.

Churchill arrived on the scene of the extraordinary "battle" in Sidney Street soon after half-past eleven, and at once took active part in the direction of the operations, consultation with the officers, the tactics of police, Scots Guards, and firemen. The Home Secretary was by no means unwilling to take risks of being hit; but was at last occupy a position less exposed than the open street. He did not leave the fighting area until three o'clock—that is to say, until after the search of the ruins of the burnt house een under siege had commenced. Thus he was present when heavy fire was being exchanged between the desperadoes and troops in the brewery and houses opposite and in the streets, when the military on duty were reinforced by a detachment with a machine gun, when the house took fire, and when Horse Artillery arrived with guns.

The scene at the 'Rising Sun'.

fourteen other City men had similar weapons, drawn from Old Jewry, and four more had small-bore Morris tube rifles from an indoor range. Later in the morning supplies were augmented on a locate-and-borrow basis; one officer drove away from a Grace-church Street gunsmith's in a taxi-cab surrounded by shotguns, rook rifles and boxes of buckshot cartridges. The London Hospital lay near the besieged house, and its chairman, the Hon. Sydney Holland, was soon among the spectators; some sporting guns were also borrowed from him.

In an indignant leader headed 'Our Defenceless Police', the *Daily Mail* dismissed the two forces' own weapons as "prehistoric" and "fit only for the museum". Their venerable shooters were certainly no match for Herr Mauser of Oberndorf's brainchild, which was the most spectacular pistol the world had ever seen. Equipped with either a ten-cartridge magazine (as in this case) or a six-cartridge one, it weighed only 2½ pounds, despite its great size;[3] the elderly revolvers were commonly about double that weight. In the German pistol the recoil was utilized to eject the empty cartridge-case and reload from the magazine; the police revolvers simply kicked like mules. Whereas each round had to be inserted individually into a revolver's rotating cylinder, one thrust of the thumb while the breech-bolt was held back charged the Mauser's magazine with the contents of a full ammunition clip. The Mauser's potential firing-rate was two shots a second or eighty aimed shots a minute, including recharging the magazine. It was especially remarkable as a weapon of precision: ordinarily sighted to 1,000 metres, it could put its 85-grain bullets within a 7-foot square at that distance.

Shortly before 9 a.m. Superintendent Mulvaney and Chief Superintendent Stark had another discussion. "It was palpable," the H Division superintendent was to write in his report, "that these men dominated the situation. . . . It was therefore decided that military aid be sought, as more effective weapons were required." Knowing how many of his force would feel about the military being brought in, Stark would have preferred to borrow

---

[3] With an overall length of 11½ inches and a 5½-inch barrel, the Mauser was also distinctive as a phallic symbol.

Service rifles for them to use; obviously, however, they were too dispersed for those who knew how to handle a rifle to be called upon.

The two officers left for Arbour Square, where Mulvaney telephoned Scotland Yard. The Commissioner, Sir Edward Henry, was out of town, but the superintendent obtained permission from Major Frederick Wodehouse, Assistant Commissioner (Administration) and Sir Edward's deputy, to apply to the 1st Battalion, Scots Guards for a detachment of marksmen. He also learned that the major was coming to Sidney Street. The Guards were stationed a mile away, at the Tower of London; Mulvaney called the Assistant Commissioner (CID), Sir Melville Macnaghten, at his home, reported the position and departed for the Tower.

Such an unprecedented state of affairs drew many important spectators. The crowds noted with respectful curiosity their arrivals by motor-car and taxi-cab. Communication between the besiegers—particularly those in front of and behind no. 100—was so difficult that effective overall direction of operations was not feasible, but Major Wodehouse reached the scene soon after nine o'clock and, nominally at least, assumed charge for a time. Macnaghten came post-haste and without his breakfast. A third Assistant Commissioner, Sir A. C. Bruce, and several chief constables also attended.

Other visitors included Sir William Nott-Bower, an Assistant Under-Secretary at the Home Office named Ernley Blackwell, and the General Officer Commanding London District, Major General Sir A. E. Codrington. Most of these special observers forgathered at the corner of Sidney Street and Lindley Street, where Macnaghten was deep in conversation with Superintendent Quinn a little while later when a ricocheting bullet tore the Special Branch chief's overcoat and severely bruised his leg. Macnaghten also visited the brewery yard, where he met Wensley; with bullets from no. 100 periodically thudding against a nearby wall, they discussed developments in the Leon Beron inquiry.[1]

---

[1] Wensley was able to give his superior encouraging news, being satisfied by this time that Morris Stein, alias Steinie Morrison, was Beron's murderer and anticipating his early arrest. During the siege he also met and talked with Detective

The Guardsmen were swabbing out their barrack rooms and doing other routine fatigues when, soon after 9.30, the bugle sounded 'Sergeant in Waiting'. A few minutes later hurrying NCOs called for volunteers. "They clamoured to get on the square," one of the many disappointed ones told the *Morning Post*. A detachment of nineteen other ranks, led by Lieutenant H. C. E. Ross and including Colour Sergeants Kitchen (a musketry instructor) and Chick, received an initial issue of ten rounds of ball ammunition per man and set out for the battlefield.

The soldiers arrived at about 10.15, a few minutes after a fire-escape sent on stand-by duty. Loud cheering greeted them as they marched along Oxford Street and into Richardson Street (immediately east of upper Sidney Street and parallel to it) in their heavy grey greatcoats, their new, short Lee-Enfield rifles at the slope and bayonets fixed.[5] After a brief conference between Lieutenant Ross, Major Wodehouse and other police officers, Kitchen, Chick and eight Guardsmen moved to positions in Sidney Street in front of the outer cordons to the north and south, about 70 yards from the besieged house. Wensley and Collinson escorted the rest of the party by roundabout routes to the brewery and nos. 109 and 111.

The idea that the two groups of Guardsmen in Sidney Street itself, lying two paces apart on mats and newspaper poster-boards placed over the muddy flagstones, should pour flanking fire on no. 100 was short-lived. It was soon obvious that, rather than helping to tighten up the siege, most of the fire of each group was simply cannoning off the Martin's Mansions frontages into the densely packed spectators behind the other.

Daily Mail reporter Frank Dilnot's experience was typical. Philip Gibbs, covering events for the *Daily Chronicle* and standing beside him at the junction of Oxford Street and Sidney Street, heard a sudden whizz and a startled exclamation; Dilnot's

Inspector Ward of W Division, the officer in charge of the Beron case and an old friend.

[5] According to some reports, it was proposed that the Guards should mount a bayonet attack on no. 100, but the idea was not pursued because of the heavy casualties anticipated and the resentment that would have been caused amongst the police.

walking-stick leaped in his hand, and a spent bullet dropped into the gutter. After a dozen minor casualties and providential escapes had occurred, the soldiers on the flanks were confined to watching for any major activity at no. 100's windows or an attempt to break out. At such a distance and so extreme an angle, even this modification was dangerous enough, as Dilnot demonstrated for *Mail* readers the following morning:

> . . . a corporal among the Guards emitted something which sounded like "Hipe!" and suddenly all the Guardsmen flung themselves on the boards and were glancing along their rifles at a head which had been thrust from a second-floor window some 80 yards along Sidney Street on the right. It was not from the assassins' house but was close to it. Fortunately the soldiers held their fire.

When the repeated ricochets finally caused the knot of reporters which included Gibbs and Dilnot to be ordered back, they entered the 'Rising Sun', a public house on the north-west corner of the junction. Here the landlord let them up on the roof for a sovereign a head. A powerful description of Gibbs's view from this eyrie appeared in his paper next morning:[6]

> It was an astounding scene. At both ends of Sidney Street the Scots Guards were in position, taking cover behind the angle of the houses. Around them were groups of policemen in uniform armed with shot-guns, and numbers of plainclothes detectives with heavy revolvers. In the shadow of doorways and archways, men crouched down with barrels of rifles and pistols pointed towards that house next to the doctor's surgery, with its shattered window-panes and broken brickwork. Looking down into the backyards of the houses opposite Martin's Buildings, I could see soldiers and armed police-men moving about, climbing over fences and getting up tall ladders so that they could fire between the chimney-pots.
>
> On the roof of [the brewery] were scores of the work-people, and as far as the eye could see across the sloping roofs, the chimney-pots and parapets, the skyline was black with heads, while in the streets below, as far as ¼ mile away, there were vast and tumultuous crowds kept back by lines of mounted policemen. The voices of

---

[6] As was normal in this period, the piece was anonymous. However, the out-standing descriptive powers it reveals strongly suggest Gibbs's work; the incident of Dilnot's walking-stick is referred to, and other evidence exists to make the possibility of someone else having written it very remote indeed.

those many thousands came up to me in great murmurous gusts, like the roar of wild beasts in a jungle. It seemed as if the whole of London had poured into Whitechapel and Stepney to watch one of the most deadly and thrilling dramas that has ever happened in the great city within living memory.

14. The Vigorous Young Statesman

The posting of Guardsmen in the brewery and the two houses opposite no. 100 marked the beginning of the end of the wanted men's desperate adventure. Joined by Kitchen, and with more ammunition, the four sharpshooters nearly 100 feet up in Mann, Crossman & Paulin's upper bottling-department and cooling-tower quickly rendered the attic room untenable. Their disciplined and accurate snap-shooting, then transferred to the second-floor windows, helped drive their adversaries downstairs once more and bring them within close range of the upstairs front rooms of nos. 109 and 111.

The soldiers in the brewery, who fired through louvred shutters from improvised vantage-points on ladders or among the casks of beer, found little enough to aim at. As Kitchen confided to the *Morning Post*:

> The assassins had the blind down, and from where I was, 60 yards away, you couldn't see into the room at all. Directly the blind moved, we blazed away on the offchance of hitting something, and when we saw the smoke of a pistol, we all banged away. If the men had come to the centre of the window to shoot, we should have nabbed them as sure as fate, but they were very wideawake and experts at taking cover. Nobody really saw anything of them—they kept close to the wall and fired around the framework of the window.

Although some newspapermen wrote about the besieged men's thirst for blood, their purpose seems in fact to have been confined to showing their contempt for the law and forcing it to keep its distance. During the ascendancy which they enjoyed between their opening volley and those of Lieutenant Ross's men, a three-hour period when one competent marksman with a cool head could have picked off any number of policemen, neither inflicted a single serious injury. Their behaviour suggests manic exaltation rather than murderous determination.

Their energy was prodigious. Thousands of spectators, having witnessed their frenetic dodging from floor to floor and window to window, left the scene convinced that there had been at least three of them. In particular, they would countenance no demonstration of superior power and were determined to match bullet for bullet, answering especially hotly the withering fire directed upon them from nos. 109 and 111. Nor, as Kitchen found, did their fanaticism blind them to the laws of self-preservation. While still clinging to their attic room, all that might occasionally be glimpsed of them—from closer quarters than the brewery—was half a face, a shirt-sleeved arm and a powder-blackened hand. Driven downstairs, they usually fired from the back of the rooms so that neither flash nor smoke could be seen.

Loosing off their bullets in the general direction of an intended target was now all that could be done. Even this called for daring, speed and skill of a high order; "A hundred times," reporter Harry Leatherdale told *Daily Express* readers, "they must have been within a hair's-breadth of death." Sometimes they seemed to be firing from the upper corners of the windows, presumably standing beside them on chairs. Occasionally a volley would be immediately preceded by the appearance of a hand holding a pistol, or simply of a muzzle protruding over the sill. Tiny movements of the lace curtains, now tattered and begrimed, could also betray the presence of a Mauser's long, thin barrel; as all the window-panes were long since shattered and the snow had been succeeded by a brisk easterly wind, however, a fluttering curtain or twitching blind proved an unreliable guide. The intermittent lulls gave way instantly to fierce exchanges of fire whenever either side detected, or thought it detected, impending hostile action.

The pair were often overheard, especially by the policemen in no. 98, shouting hoarsely to each other. The shooting did not distract them from guarding their stronghold against invasion. Some time between eight and nine o'clock, one of them shut and bolted the street door. Keeping well in against the front walls, a Detective Constable Piercey sidled up to it and, amid cheers from onlookers, smashed it open again with the butt of a rifle. This was shortly before the Guards arrived; later one of the men crept down and closed it once more. From time to time both men also fired deterrent shots towards the policemen concealed behind no. 100 and the Guardsmen and police further up and down Sidney Street.

Naturally enough, nos. 100, 109 and 111 sent and suffered the bulk of the two thousand or so rounds of ammunition fired.[1] In sharp contrast to the human congestion around it, the street in front of Martin's Mansions was bare and deserted; one newsman wrote of it being crossed and recrossed by "a hurricane of lead". Hostilities began promptly on Carl Cohen's and Isaac Dickholtz's premises; whereas most other windows directly across the road were (and remained) tightly shuttered, the first light of day found theirs with blinds down, sashes slightly raised and the muzzles of Metropolitan Police revolvers peeping beneath them.

To the besieged, the besiegers' fire had at first been a spasmodic and largely ill-directed irritant; later, when they had been forced down to its level and it had been strengthened by professional marksmen using weapons of precision, it tormented them. The exchanges across the 15 yards of empty street then acquired a special volume and venom.

"They let the rascals have it hot," was Dickholtz's comment to the *Daily Chronicle* about the Guardsmen's fire from no. 111. A military élite amongst aliens, they took over the two houses without ceremony. Harry Leatherdale described this particular sector:

> A sofa was flung on its side by the [Cohens'] sitting-room window, and the Guardsmen . . . knelt in the shelter of the sofa with their

[1] Replying to a Commons question on 16th February, the Secretary of State for War (R. B. Haldane) stated that the military fired a total of five hundred rounds. The total number fired by policemen from all types of weapon probably exceeded a thousand. The two fugitives seem to have fired at least four hundred.

Service rifles gleaming on the window-ledge by the side of the brickwork, which was already scored with the marks of revolver bullets.

Chairs, tables and other furniture were hurled into the passage so that the soldiers might have room for their work, and a heavy mirror was dragged by the side of the sofa to provide some additional protection for the kneeling men.

A civilian, armed with a six-chambered revolver, took his stand by the side of the window, ready to fire into the house at the first sign of an arm or a head. Next to him was a superintendent of the City Police in plain clothes, with a muffler round his neck and a bowler hat on his head, nursing on his knee a double-barrelled sporting gun.[2]

This was the strange scene in this little room, hung as it was with the pictures of the late King Edward and the blazoned certificates of Jewish religious leagues, such as may be found in a thousand similar homes in this alien quarter of London.

The scene in the bedroom next door was not less remarkable. Mattresses were torn from the springs and piled against the windows, and lying sprawling on them were a number of soldiers in their shirtsleeves, so that their uniforms might not draw the fire of the murderers, and with the glistening barrels of their rifles projecting from the window. . . .

To the left of the Guardsmen in the bedroom, two policemen covered the other window. One knelt beside a table which had been pushed to the side in front of the window, while the other leaned across it.

The introduction of sporting guns into the battle aptly symbolized the attitude of many besiegers. Few of them, or among the thousands of excited onlookers, seem to have thought of the two frantic young aliens as human beings. There were exceptions, however, to this tendency to view matters as a scarlet-coated huntsman. No doubt with the intention of ensuring prompt attention for any casualties, Wensley conducted Dr Johnstone and Dr D. L. Thomas, Stepney's Medical Officer of Health, to rooms opposite no. 100 in which Guardsmen were blazing away. Dr Thomas found this environment so distasteful that, after a bullet had embedded itself in the wall behind him, he retired to watch the rest of the engagement from the roof of Dickholtz's

---

[2] In reality both the "civilian" and the "superintendent" were probably inspectors.

stables. The moral issue troubled him a great deal. "When you come to think of the matter seriously," he remarked to the *Morning Post* later, "it was really lynch law."

A few minutes before eleven o'clock, two hours after Super-intendent Mulvaney's telephone call to Scotland Yard, news of the siege reached the Home Secretary himself. Winston Churchill, at home in Eccleston Square and taking a bath at the time, received a message from the Home Office with an inquiry: could the War Office be given retrospective authority for a detachment of twenty Scots Guards to proceed to the aid of the police? Churchill at once telephoned the Home Office, provided the formal sanction required, dressed and breakfasted hastily and left for Whitehall.

Little could be learned there except that (as he put it later in court) "there was a regular fusillade going on in Stepney". With such melodramatic events taking place so near at hand, the vigorous young statesman[3] was not the man to sit quietly behind a desk awaiting reports. "An extraordinary situation was evi-dently in existence," he explained, "and I thought it my duty to go and see for myself what was happening." With his private secretary, Edward Marsh, he was soon *en route* for the battlefield.

Author Gerald Bullett was later to convey the predominant attitude to the siege in a single word when he wrote of Churchill going to watch the "show".[4] If Churchill really believed that a Home Secretary and political figure of his eminence and character could attend such a public spectacle and remain a mere onlooker, he proved himself wrong from the moment—11.50— that he stepped out of his motor-car in Richardson Street. Stick in hand, top-hatted and wearing a fur-lined overcoat with a heavy astrakhan collar, his appearance alone marked him out. Many of his movements, presumably made to see everything for himself rather than rely on the word of others, attracted equally wide attention; he often strolled, apparently casually, into lines of fire

[3] Churchill had his thirty-sixth birthday on 30th November 1910. He was made a Privy Councillor in May 1907, when thirty-two, and given the Home Office at thirty-five. Only one Home Secretary had ever been younger—Sir Robert Peel, thirty-three.

[4] Gerald Bullett, *Great Unsolved Crimes* (Hutchinson, 1935), p. 225.

and had to be—to borrow *The Times*'s words—"prevailed upon to seek a more sheltered situation".

In the light of his strenuous opposition to the Aliens Bills of 1904 and 1905,[5] a naïve pleasantry attributed to Churchill when he arrived was particularly unfortunate. "Who could have imagined a scene like this in England?" the *Daily Telegraph* recorded him as exclaiming. Frustrated advocates of sterner measures for dealing with alien immigration lost no time assuring Press and public that they could have done so.

Reporters and photographers made for the newcomer with almost indecent haste; the operator of Gaumont's cinematograph machine devoted plenty of footage to him.[6] He would certainly have made a tempting target if the wanted men had not lost their command of the situation before his arrival.

Churchill spent most of his three-hour visit to Stepney either on the Sidney Street–Lindley Street corner or in a yard gateway 50 yards or so north of no. 100 and across the road from it. He seems to have been, as *The Times* aptly put it, "full of resourceful suggestion". Like the senior police officers present, he was torn between the desire that the affray be ended before nightfall and a determination to avoid the heavy casualties any attempt to rush no. 100 must bring. Approached about calling for volunteers for a rush, he proposed that some steel shields be improvised to enable the house to be reached in safety.[7] He later disowned a number of other ideas for which his authorship had been claimed.

Many newspapermen on the spot assumed that the Home Secretary had taken charge of the besieging forces. This is easily understood. In a piece headed 'How Mr Churchill Took Charge: Orders to the Police and Soldiers', Charles E. Hands of the *Daily*

---

[5] Churchill was prominently concerned in the former's abandonment. The latter passed into law as the Aliens Act of that year; it is summarized in Part III.

[6] A bioscope film of the battle was first shown at the Coliseum at 5.30 that afternoon, and at the Hippodrome, the Alhambra and other halls in the evening. Posters referred to Churchill's "directing operations" in the "danger zone".

[7] Nothing came of this at once, but a Home Office letter of 18th February 1911 to the Metropolitan Police sanctioned the expenditure of £100 for the development and purchase of such shields. (P.R.O./148/16, 17.)

Mail was categorical: "Mr Churchill at once took command of the operations. He called his generals round him in consultation, inquired after . . . the wounded officer and ascertained the disposition of the forces and the arrangements made for keeping the general public out of the line of fire. He directed that the pressing crowds be kept back and had a long, grave talk with Superintendent Mulvaney."

Major Wodehouse left to visit the War Office just before Churchill arrived, and the two men never met during the siege. Some Press reports about the Home Secretary's behaviour were probably coloured by anti-Government bias, but the Liberal *Daily Chronicle* cannot be suspected of this. A *Chronicle* man watching from the yard of a shoeing-forge across the street from the besieged house and about 25 yards north of it wrote:

> Then Mr Churchill took charge of the siege operations. He stood out in the street, although the bullets were flying wildly up and down. He motioned the line backward and took four or five of the Scots Guards a few yards nearer the house and directed their fire. He walked across to Lindley Street and had a consultation with the [two] Chief Commissioners.[8] As a result of this consultation, one of the Guardsmen was sent over into the yard in which we were standing, and he began to fire in at the ground-floor windows of the house.
>
> All this time Mr Churchill, who had lighted a cigar, was watching the scene. Now and then he would give an order, telling this line to advance or that to retire. Noticing the side door of our yard to be open, he shouted "Close that door, or you will be shot."

After assessing the position in front of the besieged house, the Home Secretary embarked on a personal tour. "I made it my business," he wrote afterwards in a letter to the court, ". . . to go round the back of the premises and satisfy myself that there was no chance of the criminals effecting their escape through the intricate area of walls and small houses at the back of

---

[8] Actually probably Mulvaney and Stark. Nott-Bower wrote in his memoirs that, while he was standing in the gateway favoured by the Home Secretary, "Mr Churchill made some suggestion to me as to possible action by the police. I replied that I was not there in any position of authority, as Sidney Street was within the jurisdiction of the Metropolitan Police, whose Assistant Commissioner was in charge. . . ." (*Op. cit.*, p. 243.)

100 Sidney Street."[9] His subordinates had of course guarded amply against this possibility many hours before.

15. An Unexpected Development

The crowds were at first made up largely of Stepney's principal inhabitants, the alien and the English labourer. Later, as news of the battle spread like wildfire across London, thousands of would-be spectators converged on the commonplace East End street.

Excitement in the City, where a proprietorial concern was felt about the outcome, brought many businesses to a standstill. Jubilee Street, late home of the Anarchist Club and the next main thoroughfare east of Sidney Street connecting the Mile End Road with the Commercial Road, thronged with taxi-cabs setting down fares in tall hats and dark coats from the City and West End; train, tram and omnibus services were disrupted by a flood of humbler visitors. Arriving by way of the Commercial Road at about 10.45, Frank Dilnot had to abandon his taxi-cab and force his way northwards along Sidney Street for more than 100 yards to reach the outer cordon. Hundreds of workers went without their midday meal to visit the scene.

East Enders were creatures quite outside the experience of many middle-class newsmen and onlookers, and this ignorance bred some irrational suspicions. Describing the often uncouth but essentially good-natured multitude as a cosmopolitan one containing many suspicious-looking characters, *The Times* wrote darkly about friends of Anarchism ready to assist the besieged men. This morbid preoccupation with a lurking menace was exceptional, however.

[9] Randolph S. Churchill, *Winston S. Churchill*: Volume II, *Young Statesman, 1901–14* (Heinemann, 1966), p. 408.

The slightest move in aid of the two fugitives would certainly have led to violence. "It was clear," commented the *Morning Post*, "that the people desired the speedy capture of the miscreants dead or alive, and if there were any sympathizers with Anarchists present, they kept discreetly silent." The surging crowds, though often bewildered and mostly subdued, cheered every development which seemed to enhance the prospects of the authorities or diminish the wanted men's. Indignant comment could be heard on all sides, and there were many displays of patriotism; a call for "three cheers for Old England" brought a rousing response.

The general bewilderment was intensified by the inability of the arena to accommodate so vast an audience; it is doubtful if one so-called spectator in ten gained more than the sketchiest idea of the course of events. Curiosity, with ignorance of the injury a whizzing bullet could cause and the range of some of the weapons in use, led to enormous risks being lightly taken. Women and children leaned out of upstairs windows; men clambered up lamp-posts, stretched out over parapets and clung to chimneys. A hoarding in Russell Street, running parallel with upper Sidney Street immediately to the west, was so suicidal a vantage-point that the police were obliged to cordon off that part of the street. One intrepid character shinned up a 40-foot drainpipe. Children ventured out of front doorways and had to be pulled back, sometimes by the armed policemen concealed in them.

With closely packed masses of eager spectators only about 100 yards to the north and south of no. 100, others to east and west in adjoining streets and so little heed for personal safety, it is remarkable that the battle brought not a single civilian casualty of any consequence. A group of London Hospital nurses stood by but had little to do. The outer cordons broke periodically; soldiers and sailors in the crowds were called upon to reinforce them. Occasionally a sudden commotion would indicate that someone had been hit. Most watchers, however, never had the chance to run much risk. Quite a number were attracted to the roofs of two public houses on the far side of the Mile End Road; here they were almost 250 yards from the besieged house, of which only the roof could be seen. Some enthusiasts paid half a sovereign to occupy roofs from which it turned out not to be visible at all.

If most people could see very little, there was plenty to hear. "The crowd heard more shots in the course of a few moments," the *Morning Post* remarked, "that many a man in South Africa during the war." Gibbs's *Daily Chronicle* account also gave a vivid idea of the noise of battle:

> [It] was tremendous and almost continuous. The heavy, barking reports of Army rifles were followed by the sharp and lighter cracks of pistol shots. Some of the weapons had a shrill, singing noise, and others were like children's pop-guns. Most terrible and deadly in sound was the rapid fire of the Scots Guards, shot speeding on shot, as though a Gatling gun were at work. Then there would come a sudden lull, as though a bugle had sounded 'Cease fire', followed by a silence, intense and strange after the ear-splitting din.

W. Holt White of the *Daily Express* noted some of the other sounds that punctuated one of these oppressive pauses: the hoarse cries from the more distant crowds, a barrel-organ playing 'Let's All Go Down The Strand', a baby wailing and the crowing of a cock.

Not surprisingly, rumour was rife amongst the crowds: several policemen had been killed; there were not two Anarchists in the blockaded house but four, even six; one of them was a woman, and another was definitely Peter the Painter; they had some explosives; a loud noise was no. 100 being knocked down. When two policemen escorted a resentful pickpocket through a mass of people, he was at once assumed to be one of the wanted men. Leeson was widely believed to have died in hospital, and a story that Wensley had been shot was printed in some evening papers. Later on, it was said that the fugitives had broken through into an adjoining house, also that they had escaped through a secret tunnel.

Reporters drew freely on the human touches amidst the high drama. An old woman two houses from the besieged one appeared now and again at her front door, arms folded under her apron, seemingly quite unconcerned; another woman watched from a window through tortoiseshell-handled lorgnettes. Many newly washed garments strung across the yards behind no. 100 acquired bullet-holes. Two plain-clothes men stood nonchalantly in no. 98's top-floor window at the height of the siege, observing the firing from a dozen different quarters.

Outside, famished policemen ate and drank whenever and whatever they could. One was seen to bring out a paper bag and share five small buns with his friends; a kind-hearted Polish family distributed bread and butter and hot coffee amongst one of the outer cordons; a baker on the corner of Richardson Street and Hawkins Street did a brisk trade in cheese sandwiches with them. A great many just went hungry.

An elderly postman was determined to deliver letters a few doors from the besieged house; accompanied by several policemen and with stray bullets whistling around, he was permitted to do so. A pair of linesmen sent out early in the morning to a telegraph pole in the brewery yard realized what an irresistible target they would make if they climbed it, took cover and waited philosophically for peace. Two incandescent lamps in Sidney Street glowed feebly all day, it having proved too dangerous to put them out.

Keeping the guns opposite the wanted men's refuge provided with ammunition was a risky business. W. Wilson Ruttle of the *Daily Express* recorded how individual police volunteers would make sudden diagonal rushes across the road from the northern corner of Martin's Mansions carrying cartridges in their capes. "One was a stout man who could scarcely effect a run," Ruttle wrote, "and at any other time the spectacle would have been almost laughable. Now he was transformed into a hero, and the onlookers painfully held their breaths until he reached safety."

Around noon, Stepney's dull grey roofs glistened in unexpected sunshine. Harry Leatherdale described an incident which occurred during a lull at this time—the improvisation, at Lieutenant Ross's suggestion, of a dummy uniformed policeman that might tempt the fugitives to reveal themselves. When this effigy, complete with helmet, was raised in Cohen's first-floor sitting-room window, it drew fire immediately. The bullet missed the dummy, bounced off the gilded ceiling gaselier and hit a policeman on the hand. There was a hiss of escaping gas. The injured man was taken to Dr Krestin, who was downstairs.

"Between 12 and 12.30," recorded the *Morning Post*, "there is a perfect hurricane of shots on both sides." This half-hour marked the peak of the fugitives' resistance. Then, at 12.50, came a completely unexpected development. During one of the uneasy breathing spaces, hazy smoke was seen to be rising from one of no. 100's chimneys and oozing out of the second-floor windows, particularly the stockroom one at the back. Many onlookers at once concluded that the authorities had decided to burn the house down. Would its occupants make a dash for freedom? The continuous murmur of the crowds rose expectantly, and loud cheering was heard.

The advent of fire brought yet another unprecedented situation. Mulvaney himself sent for the brigade. Mile End Road fire-station received the call at 1.3, and within five minutes a horsed escape with Sub-Officer Drew in charge was less than 150 yards north of the besieged house. So far, the thick wedge of humanity had impeded it; now a police inspector forbade Drew to proceed further. Drew stopped the 'steamer' (steam-operated fire-engine) which had followed up his appliance, told Station Officer Edmonds, who was on it, that the police were "smoking out burglars" and passed on the instruction that the fire was not to be put out at present.

Edmonds saw this as pure heresy. The inspector declined to argue and referred him to the Home Secretary. Churchill had by this time returned to the corner of Lindley Street, where he was deep in consultation with Stark and Mulvaney. Grim-faced, Edmonds forced his way down Sidney Street and strode over to them. He knew nothing about the siege and was surprised to hear gunfire. When he bearded the three men, he was told that if he approached the house he would probably be shot, and the order was confirmed.

Churchill crossed Sidney Street once more to the gateway for a better view of the fire's progress. As time passed, galloping horses and clanging bells told of the arrival of other appliances, some north of no. 100 and some south; all were ordered to bring their engines near and be prepared to prevent the outbreak from spreading. "Perhaps for the first time in the history of the London Fire-Brigade," the *Morning Post* observed, "the brass-helmeted men stand idly by with their apparatus watching the flames grow without any attempt to extinguish them." Edmonds and his men were obliged to do so for more than an hour.

One of the
Mauser pistols
used in Sidney
Street.

In a bedroom
opposite no. 100.

The siege ends . . .

. . . and the crowds close in.

There was another diversion at one o'clock when Colour Sergeant Chick, who had survived seven engagements with the Boers, became the first and only military casualty. He and his colleagues were lying in the roadway watching for activity at the windows, the sergeant said afterwards, and had just "let drive" when he was hit. Some Guardsmen attributed the bullet, which grazed his calf, to one of the wanted men's deterrent shots at the outer cordons, but watchers at the other end of Martin's Mansions could well have just let drive too. Chick was taken to the London Hospital in Churchill's motor-car. His subsequent return to duty brought hearty cheers, as did the firemen's arrival.

The crowd's elation at the prospect of a fire inside no. 100 soon gave way to disappointment at its slow progress. No flames appeared. The east wind was dying down, and the smoke, likened by Gibbs to that of "a damp bonfire which has not yet begun to blaze", shrouded the top floor in a dense veil. As its volume slowly increased, it turned from white to grey and from grey to black. Presently, at about 1.20, tiny scraps of burned and unburned paper began to be wafted up in it.

The besiegers had met this ominous turn of events by intensifying their attack. Although the shooting from no. 100 still continued, the stabs of flame from the fugitives' weapons sometimes being visible through the thickening smoke, their defiance was evidently nearing its end. Also at about 1.20, smoke began to seep through the first-floor windows, suggesting that the fire had penetrated the floor above. Firemen in Sidney Street prepared stand-pipes and unreeled hose to within 50 yards of the burning house.

At about 1.30 a second and larger detachment of Scots Guards received the usual effusive welcome. This consisted of three officers—Captain W. J. Wickham, his brother, Lieutenant J. L. Wickham, and Lieutenant E. B. Trafford—and fifty-one other ranks. These men, who carried a hundred rounds of ball ammunition apiece, were marched into a yard behind the west side of Sidney Street and drawn on as reliefs and reinforcements. With them came more ammunition in boxes and a Lee-Metford machine-gun on a hand-cart. Onlookers watched the machine-gun detail mount it on its tripod and fill the ammunition belts.

Also at 1.30, by which time the first-floor smoke had become ominously dark and heavy, the crowds noted with enthusiasm that flames were licking the woodwork of the front attic window. A quarter of an hour later there could be no doubt that fire had a firm grip on the top three floors.

The position of no. 98's occupants—who included Mrs Krestin, her four children and a serving-maid—now seemed perilous. Several of the Krestins' back windows were extremely close to those of no. 100. Flames could be seen rearing angrily out of no. 100's roof and upper back windows; the blaze at the front was reflected in window-panes across the street. Smoke was finding its way into no. 98's upstairs rooms. The party walls in Martin's Mansions were fireproofed, but it is unlikely that the policemen in the Krestins' house knew of this. Mrs Krestin was told to gather up her children and valuables and leave at once. W. R. Holt of the *Daily Mail* watched the flight to safety in Hawkins Street:

> An anxious woman ran out of the door, a baby in her arms, and a plainclothes officer with a loaded revolver took her by the waist and raced up the street. Two or three other women and children followed, running as fast as they could, under the protection of men with pistols who pushed them forward. A fussy little servant-maid with red hair and a blue gown took her chance twice, running back for a parcel . . . which she had forgotten. That was at the very moment when the sharpshooters had their guns pointed at the yard door [to no. 98, which was in Hawkins Street] she had to pass.

16. The Kill

Realizing that the besieged men's refuge was likely to be burned to the ground around them, many hitherto callous people grew anxious about their ultimate fate. The *Daily Telegraph*, certainly not soft-hearted towards them, recorded an awed feeling that the young aliens might be lying wounded, to be burned to death, or facing the terrible decision whether to perish inside or take their chances with the eager trigger-fingers outside. Nevertheless, the police made no attempt to suggest capitulation to them. The official explanation for this omission was summed up by Mulvaney in his report: ''It will be borne in mind that it was open to these men at any time to leave the burning house and surrender by coming into the street without their weapons and putting their hands up in the usual manner. . . .'' The *Telegraph* on the other hand was certain that, if they had come out, the soldiers would have shot them down; and *The Times* considered that in the indiscriminate firing some spectators would probably have shared their fate. Apart from the military, there were many individual policemen blazing away from isolated points of vantage. It was probably as well for the reputation of British justice that the official proposition never came to be tested.

By this time Assistant Divisional Officer Morris had advised the Home Secretary that the fire might soon spread to the whole of Martin's Mansions, and four more steamers were ordered up. The chief officers of the London Fire-Brigade and the Salvage Corps were soon on the scene.

The smoke masking the front of the stricken house and the fevered imaginations of the onlookers combined to bring about at least one hallucination. This was at 1.40, when hundreds of people were horrified to see what appeared to be the blackened figure of a man who had climbed out of one of the second-floor windows and was crouching on the ledge. Seconds later, after this apparition had drawn its quota of bullets, the smoke thinned; it was a curtain bellied out by a strong draught.

Another widely reported incident, at about the same time and in the same room, may well have been significant. A hand holding a pistol was seen in front of the curtain to the left-hand window. Two shots from the pistol were answered immediately by two volleys from the brewery. The hand fell and disappeared.

The last shots from the front of the burning house were fired from the ground-floor window at 1.50. The floors above were ablaze by this time, and any escape into Sidney Street would obviously have to take place within minutes. Fingers tightened on triggers. Guardsmen and uniformed policemen with shot-guns advanced warily; detectives with revolvers started to leave cover. The soldiers and policemen in nos. 109 and 111, who had been joined by Kitchen, watched tensely. But the front door on which all eyes were fixed remained closed.

Gibbs's description of no. 100's death-throes was a Wagnerian *tour de force* about fire-demons, blazing timbers, crashing masonry, whirlwinds of dancing sparks and the devilish games of fury played by the flames. Meanwhile, Churchill had returned to the Lindley Street corner for more discussions. He and his group, which included Superintendent Quinn and Detective Chief Inspector McCarthy (also of the Special Branch), then recrossed Sidney Street to the yard of the shoeing-forge. Here the Home Secretary was again watched by the unknown *Daily Chronicle* reporter:

> The Guardsman who was with us knelt to fire, and Mr Churchill stooped down and directed his aim. "Fire at the door," he said, and the bullet crashed across the street at point-blank range, and a shower of splinters showed that it had found its mark. Then Mr Churchill motioned to one of the policemen with a shot-gun to come forward, and he too fired two more shots into the ground-floor windows.
>
> By this time the house itself was a roaring mass of flame from top to bottom. . . . Then he gave orders to open wide the doors of the yard, so that those inside could take uninterrupted aim should there be a bolt down the street.

The absurdity of continuing to pour lead into such a conflagration was obvious, and at two o'clock, by a common decision, the besiegers held their fire. It was inconceivable that any human being in the front of the house could still be alive.

Unused ammunition crackled in the fire. Accompanied by two fellow plain-clothes officers and keeping close in to the wall like Detective Constable Piercey, the burly McCarthy picked his way through the debris to the scarred front door. He kicked it open, but licking flames and pungent smoke made entry beyond the hall impossible. Hurriedly, his top hat on the back of his head and a police sergeant with a double-barrelled shotgun at his side, Churchill walked along the pavement to a point opposite the fire-swept house. Four Guardsmen and several armed policemen, weapons at the ready, took up positions in front of Dickholtz's yard.

A whistle was blown, and a dozen firemen, also escorted by armed policemen, came slowly forward with their hoses. Most of them began pouring water into the blaze at once from ground level; three climbed the escape to the top of the building, and others attached a hooked ladder to one of the first-floor window-sills. "The water from the hose comes stinging down like rain," W. R. Holt told *Daily Mail* readers. "Mr Churchill's hat is ruined. He converses eagerly with high officials. Armed policemen stand around him." Just before 2.30 the firemen were able to enter the house itself through the front door.

While the flames ravaged the storeys overhead, there had also been shooting from the rear of the ground floor. Policemen behind no. 100 saw movements periodically and fired at them. At about 2.5 a *Times* reporter watched a fireman cross the yard of no. 98 and climb on the wall separating it from the yard of no. 100. "The few who saw his cool advance," wrote the reporter, "held their breath in tense anxiety." The fireman sat nonchalantly on the wall a few feet from the middle room window for several minutes, looking up at the blaze and adjusting the nozzle of his hose.

The onlookers' qualms were justified. After the firemen had begun work at the front of the house, Sergeant Thurlow heard four more shots fired from the back and noticed the compression the bullets caused crossing the yard through the damp air. Hose had been run out along Hawkins Street, and other firemen were about to enter the yard behind no. 3. Thurlow warned them about this last volley, and no further move was made for a time. When they finally ventured out and crossed the intervening walls, no more shooting occurred. Thurlow went with them, and their intrepid lone colleague joined them. Finding Rebecca's kitchen swamped but almost untouched by the fire, this party was first into the house.

The kitchen's proper occupant was herself far from unscathed. Crowded into the middle ground-floor room of no. 102, with its barricaded window and remnants of Christmas decorations, no. 100's refugees bemoaned their fate. A *Daily Chronicle* reporter described the scene as "a pathetic [one] of squalor and hysterics, and noisy with a perpetual babble of Yiddish protest". Rebecca was too full of anguish about losing her home, her furniture and her beautiful jewellery and not having even a stocking to her feet to tell him much.

Surrounded by senior officials, Churchill stood near no. 100's doorstep watching the firemen. Filthy flotsam from the front room—the twisted remnants of a brass bedstead, a battered tin bath, a Singer sewing-machine, charred fragments of furniture and much sodden and smouldering bedding—was thrown or handed through the gaping window-socket and began to pile up on the pavement. Items removed from the back of the house included a dressmaker's dummy and an ornately carved rocking-cradle.

At 2.40, when it was evident that no one in the house had survived, Churchill drove off to a City restaurant for lunch. As he did so, a section of Royal Horse Artillery trotted up. This formidable reinforcement—two quick-firing 13-pounder guns with limbers and waggons and twenty rounds of shrapnel—was from BB Battery's barracks in St John's Wood; the 6-mile journey across London had been accomplished, it was said, in forty minutes and without drawing rein. Many who stopped to watch the turn-out clatter by guessed its destination; it was warmly cheered *en route*, when it arrived and when it left. The disappointed artillerymen stayed until 3.15, their glossily elegant horses and immaculate equipment drawing an admiring audience of solemn-eyed East End children.

A systematic search for the two bodies was started shortly before three o'clock. About ten firemen set to work. Nothing was discovered in the front ground-floor room but, almost as soon as the task of transferring debris from the middle room to the back yard began, Station Officer Clarke (from Globe Road station in Bow) noticed a "bulky mass" lying practically on top of the debris about 3 feet from the fireplace. This proved to be a charred human torso. Two children's books lay nearby.

The H Division surgeon, Dr Charles Graham Grant, was brought to examine the find. "It was burned beyond all recognition," he told the court. Three plain coffins were delivered at about 3.30, and one of them, with the torso inside and tied up with string, was taken to Stepney mortuary on a hose-cart with a tarpaulin over it.

Clarke's find had first been removed to an outhouse, and just after this a sudden collapse overhead resulted in injury to five of the firemen searching the middle room. Inspector Wensley, who was close at hand, had a narrow escape. Three other firemen were unhurt; one of them told W. Holt White of the *Daily Express*:

> I was nearest the door, next to me was Mr [District Officer] Pearson and, beyond him against the wall, Mr [Superintendent] Canning. There was suddenly a crackling, rumbling sound overhead. Mr Pearson shouted "Push out, there's something going to fall," and as he spoke he shoved me forward. I fell face foremost through the door, and as I did so a hearthstone from the top floor crashed through and pinned Mr Pearson down. My feet were caught beneath his head. I struggled out somehow and turned back to give him a hand.
>
> The hearthstone, a great heavy thing about 8 inches thick and weighing perhaps 2 hundredweight, was burning hot, and it was no easy matter to lift it off him. The other men were injured by bricks and falling beams brought down by the hearthstone.

A rescue party extricated the victims. "It was a piteous sight," said the *Daily Chronicle*, "to see these brave fellows, half-smothered and black with smoke and dust, and with bleeding hands and faces, being carried out on the arms of their comrades." First to emerge were Canning and three firemen, who were driven to the London Hospital in a salvage waggon, all but their faces covered with tarpaulins. Last of all came Pearson, who, still unconscious, was rushed away on an improvised ambulance. The spectators, many of whom concluded that the five had fallen to the fugitives' bullets, showed sympathy by cheering them; there was great indignation, and several women were moved to tears.

By the time the Scots Guards marched away, also amid cheers, the pale January sun was throwing long shadows across Sidney Street. After the hearthstone incident a fireman mounted the escape and dislodged dangerous projections with a long hook. The LCC's District Surveyor had no. 100's outside walls shored up at once, and the police arranged some shoring inside.

The search of the middle ground-floor room continued by lantern-light when darkness fell, and at intervals there were further significant finds. At about 6.30 Fireman Swain, digging 2 feet or so from the wall beneath the window, came across a skull-cap "with brains attached". There was a good deal of debris on top of this and only about one inch of it underneath; having been inspected by Dr Grant, it was put in a towel with various other fire-blackened relics recognizable as human.

An hour later, when the wreckage in the middle room was almost cleared, a fire-brigade motor-car fetched the police surgeon for a third examination. Working just inside the door, Fireman Gander had located the second body. This was practically at floor level under a great quantity of debris. The body appeared to be lying on its left side. Gander caught hold of what seemed to him to be the right forearm, and a piece about 6 inches long came away in his hands. He then set about carefully clearing away the debris surrounding the incinerated mass. A Mauser pistol lay just underneath the dead man's back near the hip. This was the second Mauser to be found, Fireman Coleman having discovered the other about one foot from this body shortly before the body itself came to light. Both pistols were on much the same, very low level of debris as the body.

"At 7.40 [Dr Grant testified later] I was called to examine another body. The forearms were gone, and the bones of the upper arms were sticking up through the debris. I pulled upon these, and by that means the body began to rise through the rubbish." The lower portion of the face, the nose and part of the orbits to the eyes were all that was left of the head. The tongue protruded from the mouth. Some burned fragments of clothing clung to the corpse; all over it, and particularly under what remained of the left arm, were patches of lead which had evidently poured down on it when molten. Under the doctor's supervision it was put into a second coffin. Four firemen shouldered the burden and carried it out through the front door; soon after eight o'clock it was on its way by ambulance to the mortuary.

PART III

Matters Arising

17. Refugees, Ruffians and the Right of Asylum

At the heart of the mightiest empire the world had ever known, 4 miles from Buckingham Palace and less than two from the Bank of England, the massed forces of law and order had been spectacularly defied by a pair of anonymous foreign desperadoes. The country was stunned.

As they had done after the Exchange Buildings outrage, Tory newspapers knew exactly where to put the blame for this *lèse majesté*—on the Aliens Act of 1905 and Radical political attitudes. A second and much heavier barrage of indignant protest was laid down at once.

The 1905 Act, Britain's first attempt to control the flow of impoverished immigrants by legislation, was a patchwork of half-measures. Other faults apart, it applied to only a tiny minority of aliens seeking entry to Britain; vessels carrying twenty or less alien steerage passengers were not regarded as immigrant ships and were exempted, as also were all cabin-class passengers, passengers passing through the country *en route* to others, holders of return tickets and crew members.[1]

Although the Act had been passed in the last months of the previous Conservative and Unionist Administration and had been framed with the destitute rather than the criminal alien in mind, it was a handy stick to belabour the Radicals with. Many of its manifold weaknesses could be fairly attributed to the mauling the Bills of 1904 and 1905 had received from Churchill and others of like mind.

There was an additional opening for attack. The Act gave the Home Secretary wide powers for regulating its operation, and

---

[1] Of the 534,805 alien passengers desiring admission to Britain in 1909, only 11,930 were submitted to the tests imposed by the Act. One in four of all these aliens—134,718—came on "twenty or less" ships.

the Liberals had succeeded to office just before it came into effect on 1st January 1906. Many people were convinced that sinister Radical influences had also undermined its administration.

Churchill's Liberal predecessor at the Home Office had been Herbert Gladstone. On 19th December 1905, only days after taking over from the last Unionist Home Secretary, Gladstone had made an order reducing the maximum permissible number of alien steerage passengers on a ship classifiable as non-immigrant from twenty to twelve. This made one of the Act's principal loop-holes much smaller, but on 9th March 1906—five days after a Commons debate in which the Act's Radical opponents had been particularly vocal—the order was cancelled.

In the Act itself was a proviso that

> . . . in the case of an immigrant who proves that he is seeking admission to this country solely to avoid prosecution or punishment on religious or political grounds or for an offence of a political character, or persecution, involving danger of imprisonment or danger to life or limb, on account of religious belief, leave to land shall not be refused on the ground merely of want of means, or the probability of his becoming a charge on the rates.

Between 1905 and 1908, Eastern Europe was in a ferment of revolutionary disorder. Also on 9th March 1906, Gladstone caused the following instruction to be sent to immigration officers: "In all cases in which immigrants, coming from the parts of the Continent which are at present in a disturbed condition, allege that they are flying from political or religious persecution, the benefit of the doubt, where any doubt exists, as to the truth of the allegation will be allowed, and leave to land will be given."[2]

Although the Act contained flaws for which the Radicals could not be held responsible, few Tory commentators were prepared to admit this. Most Tory newspapers showed far more concern about criminal immigrants than about the management of affairs in Sidney Street. "There is no longer a shadow of excuse," exclaimed the *Daily Telegraph* angrily, "for pretending not to

---

[2] Parliamentary paper Cd.2879 of 1906.

know what Anarchism means and what sort of foreign riff-raff[3] is being freely introduced into England. . . ." It would be the Government's plain duty to undo forthwith the damage Churchill and Gladstone had wrought. The *Daily Express* leader-writer was caustic: "When this present Administration was inflicted on the country," he wrote, "its first care was to whittle away [the Act's] efficiency"; this had been done "in obedience to the dictates of the heart which bleeds for the misfortunes of every country but its own". He too censured Churchill.

The Liberal Press girded itself for fresh battle. "Politicians of the baser sort," the *Daily Chronicle* commented scornfully, "will probably seek to make party capital out of the affair. The attempt will be futile." If legislation was to be blamed, it must be remembered that the Aliens Act was a Unionist measure. The *Daily News* thought that such a startling exception made an apt opportunity for praising the rule: Britain had a proud history as a shelter for political refugees.

Everybody naturally wanted to keep out "criminal lunatics like these Anarchist expropriators", the London evening *Star*'s leader-writer said, but no one could show how. Unfortunately, criminal aliens tended to look exactly like the law-abiding kind. Furthermore, since the Act confined itself to the inspection of steerage passengers, foreign criminals had only to pay a higher fare to avoid it. Having defeated an Opposition amendment to make all passengers subject to inspection, the Unionists could blame only themselves for this.

The *Star*'s arguments were hard to refute. The difference in fares on a short crossing was only a few shillings. It was generally assumed that men such as Morountzeff and Fritz Svaars would have purchased their immunity this way.

Other Press comment ranged further afield. As the *Pall Mall*

---

[3] Contempt of this sort was commonly expressed for immigrants generally. Ex-CID chief Sir Robert Anderson, seldom at a loss for an extravagant phrase, referred to Britain as "a cess-pool for the scum of creation"; Father Bernard Vaughan called her a "dust-bin for the refuse of the Continent". Several on-the-spot critics of the recent great influx of aliens into east London, including members of Stepney's Borough Council and Board of Guardians, took the opportunity to remark that whole streets of native tradesmen had been "driven out" by these immigrants, most of whom were Jews.

Gazette saw it, the Continent's "most abandoned ruffians" had been deliberately invited to call themselves political refugees and come to live in Britain. "If you let in the jungle, you must be prepared for the jungle's ways." Most steerage passengers from Eastern Europe seeking admission to Britain being Jews, the Jewish Press particularly feared tighter legislation. The *Jewish Chronicle* diagnosed the root of the trouble without hesitation: "The men who held the 'fort' in the East End were the debased and brutalized products of depraved foreign administration. . . . A piece of Russia has been transplanted to London."

The Times took a calm—if jaundiced—view of the battle itself. It felt that the police should have been able to cope without calling in the military. "We do not quite see how the ruffians were to have been captured by the procedure adopted," it mused, adding that "on a sober review of the facts . . . we are not sure that the outcome redounds very much to our credit." It was icily disapproving of the Home Secretary's presence.

The action taken in Sidney Street was wholeheartedly supported by the Paris Prefecture of Police. The words of a high official there, as translated by the *Daily Telegraph* correspondent, held a reassuring finality: "The means adopted for the reduction of such redoubtable bandits to impotence are the only ones that ought to be employed." Britain had amply demonstrated the principle that behind every British policeman stood the full power of the State.

French Press and public opinion were virtually unanimous in echoing this approval. The British Government, said *Le Temps*, had acted with rapidity, resolution and severity. Comment on Britain's attitude towards some of her immigrants was less favourable, however. Of Gladstone's benefit-of-the-doubt instruction *L'Eclair* asked: "Is it possible to give a clearer invitation to the Anarchists to come to London?" By providing a refuge for foreign insurgents on the understanding that the revolutions and assassinations they plotted should take place elsewhere, Britain had been guilty of "treachery towards the brotherhood of nations".

Britain's relations with her partner of the *Entente Cordiale* and with Kaiser Wilhelm II's Germany were in sharp contrast; Berlin reacted very differently from Paris. A *communiqué* published in the Berlin *Lokalanzeiger* on the authority of the President of Police, von Jagow, himself was fittingly described by the *Daily Telegraph* as "emptying the vials of ridicule". The "foolish right of asylum" had been responsible for Exchange Buildings and Sidney Street, von Jagow declared. The police performance in Sidney Street met with his particular contempt; it could be compared to shooting sparrows with cannon, he said.

In German military circles and most newspapers the affair produced self-congratulation and mockery. "Such a tragi-comedy as this in London," the *National-Zeitung* observed, "in which the power of the State plays so inglorious a part, would not be possible with us." The *Post* wrote sarcastically of "the besieging army commanded by the intrepid Churchill". It was a proud boast of the German police that their political organization knew more about Anarchist activities in London than Super-intendent Quinn and his colleagues,⁴ but information passed on to the London police had been rejected, the *Deutsche Tageszeitung* alleged. It hoped that the events of 3rd January would put an end to such "arrogance". The absence of any systematic co-operation between the police forces of different countries led to many suggestions that an "international vigilance bureau" of some kind be established.⁵

Predictably, Socialist publications in the two countries had other views. "Banditism from below replies to banditism from above," remarked *L'Humanité*, writing about the plight of the Jews under Russia's "atrocious régime of murder and blood". The siege was deliberately being magnified into a battle with Anarchists, *Vorwaerts* asserted, in the hope that the right of asylum might be withdrawn.

Conservative newspapers in Vienna recognized Britain's

---

⁴ It would not be surprising if this claim were true. In 1910 Quinn's branch consisted of about a dozen men—scarcely comparable with the ten commis-sioners, ten inspectors and 123 other ranks who were said to make up the staff of Berlin's political police.

⁵ Improved international co-operation led eventually to the formation of Interpol in 1923. Interpol cannot act in political, religious, racial or military cases, however, only in purely criminal ones.

peculiar difficulties: her law differed basically from Continental in presuming innocence until guilt was proved, rather than the other way about, and the power to accept or reject alien immigrants was vested in a department of State rather than the police. Next to the United Kingdom the European country most hospitable to the Russian expatriate was Switzerland; *émigrés* there were quick to condemn the Exchange Buildings and Sidney Street crimes and express anxiety about more stringent British legislation.

Reports of the Battle of Stepney published in New York were as voluminous (and sometimes as inaccurate) as Fleet Street's. "The vastness of the paraphernalia unfolded by the police"—as the *Daily Mail's* New York correspondent put it—was sometimes considered undignified, but the completeness and finality of the outcome were widely admired.

Both Churchill and the police came in for blunt criticism. "Even the old politics-ridden New York police never did a more bungling job," the *Globe* claimed. The *Evening Post* saw the siege as "a curious mixture of heroism and tomfoolery" and like Mafeking night; Churchill's attendance had been "an unnecessary piece of self-advertisement". He was "rather given to spectacular display himself," in the *Sun's* opinion. The irony of such an event occurring in the very heart of sophisticated, law-abiding Britain was not lost on several commentators.

Few governments were more sensitive to the threat of Anarchism than that of the United States, where an Act passed by Congress in 1907 expressly prohibited the admission of "Anarchists or persons who believe in or advocate the overthrow by force or violence of the Government of the United States or of all government, or of all forms of law, or the assassination of public officials." Recognition of intending immigrants of this sort was so difficult, however, that the practical value of the provision was soon proved to be negligible. Conservative circles remained apprehensive about these shadowy disciples of disorder and, as in Europe, hoped that Sidney Street would teach them a severe lesson.

Russians themselves heard little about the siege; conditioned by years of revolutionary outrage and bloodshed, they would have paid small attention to it anyway. The work of laying Anarchists and other international criminals by the heels, the police of St Petersburg complained, was seriously impeded by Britain's unhelpful attitude and the immunity they could so easily obtain there.

The Lettish Social Democratic Committee in Brussels protested at British Press reports connecting its party with the "horrible deeds" done in Exchange Buildings and Sidney Street. The 1907 Congress of the Russian Social Democratic Party had passed a special resolution forbidding members to have anything whatsoever to do with expropriators, it said, and the ban had been scrupulously enforced. The committee had no doubt that "English democracy will distinguish between criminal hooligans and convinced Socialists."

18. The Important and Conspicuous Spectator

Very few contributors to the immense public debate that followed the battle questioned its morality. "Civilization and a Browning pistol are contradictory terms," decided 'An Ordinary Man' in the *Daily Mail*, "and, civilized methods being excluded, Justice vindicated herself in the rough and ready ways of the bush or the mining camp." *The Times* printed a letter from Canon Barnett, who sought a higher moral standard in police operations: "By such a standard it would not have been possible to engage soldiers and police in shooting at two men during seven hours, in the presence of an excited mass of men and women, including fashionable people from the West End," he wrote. "Methods of barbarism—lawless action in the punishment of lawlessness— are likely to destroy respect for life and for law." Canon Barnett's strictures rankled sufficiently with Assistant Commissioner Sir Melville Macnaghten for him to recall them nearly four years later.[1] They were "simply silly", he declared; the besieged men were "wild beasts seeking to destroy, and it is the part, office and duty of police to turn the tables on all such dangers to humanity."

Equally sharp criticism from another humanitarian standpoint came from a second clergyman, the Reverend Lionel Lewis, whose vicarage overlooked the Leman Street section-house. Mr Lewis, who had seen unmarried constables roused at 4.30 a.m. and sent off to Sidney Street, wrote to *The Times* protesting that most of them had had no food between coming off duty at various times on Monday evening and 5.30 or 6.30 on Tuesday evening. Provision carts never visited the Metropolitan Police, he pointed out. To oblige policemen to combine a gruelling experience such as Sidney Street with fasts ranging from thirteen to twenty-two hours seemed "both stupid and unnecessarily cruel". Churchill's answers to two Commons questions on the subject on 13th February having failed to mollify him, Mr Lewis wrote to the Home Office disputing their accuracy in detail.[2] On 28th March, after pressing for a reply, he received a blandly dismissive one conceding nothing. He then sent the correspondence to *The Times*, which gave it generous coverage.

Whatever might be thought about the way in which the fugitives' defiance had been overcome, their courage did not pass unnoticed, least of all by the police. "They were blackguards, but they died game," a policeman remarked to the *Daily Express*; "It was impossible to help admiring the courage of the desperate ruffians," wrote Nott-Bower.[3]

More prosaic factors—the apparent incompetence of the police, the employment of the military, doubts about the legal proprieties, ignorance of many details of the battle, surprise at the Home Secretary's presence and the ambiguous part he had played—provided *The Times* with a weighty correspondence. As

[1] At the end of a brief account of the siege in his memoirs. Sir Melville L. Macnaghten, *Days of My Years* (Edward Arnold, 1914), p. 264.

[2] The questions dealt with both feeding and hours worked. The answers were brief, apparently offhand and certainly less than frank. One of them described Leman Street section-house as "close by" Sidney Street; the two were in fact about a mile apart.

[3] *Op. cit.*, p. 244.

Churchill, the only individual under criticism, allowed himself to be drawn into the controversy, the arguments centred more and more upon him as the days went by.

On Friday, 6th January, came a letter from Sir Harry Poland, KC.[4] Sir Harry agreed with *The Times* that soldiers should not be called upon to do for the police what the police were capable of doing for themselves. This had cast a "great slur" on the police, and an impartial tribunal should be set up to inquire into it. The Home Secretary had undoubtedly committed a grave error of judgment, and compromised his position, by attending.

On the same day Churchill wrote to Sir Henry Dalziel MP, a Liberal colleague. The letter was published in Sunday's *Reynolds's Newspaper*. He shared Dalziel's surprise, Churchill said in it, "that a section of our fellow-countrymen should be so ready to join in the carping and sneering criticisms of the ill-informed Continental Press". The vast majority of Englishmen had every confidence in the London police, and he would be ready to answer any criticisms of them in the House of Commons. The implication that such criticism might only be dealt with in Parliament—when it assembled in a month's time—nettled the critics, many of whom also took his letter to mean that Churchill did not consider his own part in the siege to be in question.

The whole affair had been muddled, E. H. Pickersgill MP suggested in Monday's *Times*. The trouble was that, since the Home Secretary—who had acted "very foolishly"—was responsible for the actions of the Metropolitan Police, the matter at once became party political. All the Liberal newspapers were defending the indefensible and all the Conservative ones making party capital. Rather than risk policemen's lives, the inhabitants of Sidney Street had been exposed to extreme danger. That soldiers had been firing in anger in the streets of London, and under the direction of the civil authority, was particularly disquieting.

On Tuesday the dissenters were joined by Sir Joseph West

---

[4] Sir Harry, who was eighty-one years old, had acted as counsel to the Treasury and the Home Office for many years before retiring in 1895. He was also an LCC alderman.

Ridgeway,[5] who questioned whether the legal formalities governing the use of the military had been properly complied with. Sir West considered Churchill's conduct "natural enough in a young and impetuous Minister of undoubted courage and self-confidence" but was alarmed at the precedent he had set. If he could take charge in Sidney Street, "what is to prevent a Secretary of State for War from joining an army in the field and dictating to the general in command the manner in which he should handle his troops?"

Wednesday brought another letter from Sir Harry Poland, who evidently did not share Sir West's tolerant attitude. Sir Harry wanted to know more about the various military forces detailed for duty in Sidney Street: who sent for them and why, how many were there,[6] what did they do, when did they arrive and depart? Why was no official information forthcoming? Churchill would find his own conduct harder to defend than that of the police, Sir Harry thought. He also delivered a Parthian shaft: "The following passage in Mr Winston Churchill's letter [to Dalziel] has excited some surprise: 'There are, and there ought to be, other ways of dealing with beasts of prey than by choking them in British blood.' This is hardly the quiet, calm language to be expected from a Secretary of State."

On Thursday *The Times* printed the following letter from Churchill:

> Sir,
>
> There is one respect at least in which I must disappoint the curiosity of Sir Harry Poland and rebut his charges and those of Sir Joseph West Ridgeway.

---

[5] Like Churchill, Sir West was a Privy Councillor. He was a Knight Commander of the Bath and of the Star of India, also an honorary Doctor of Laws of Cambridge and Edinburgh. He had concluded a distinguished career as Governor and Commander-in-Chief of Ceylon.

[6] The Secretary of State for War (R. B. Haldane) told the Commons on 16th February that the following troops had been detailed for service in Sidney Street: Scots Guards, four officers and seventy NCOs and men; Royal Horse Artillery, one officer and thirty-four NCOs and men; Royal Engineers, three officers and twelve NCOs and men. It seems that the Engineer party was ordered up from Chatham with the idea of using explosives on no. 100 but turned back after the house had caught fire.

I did not assume the direction of events in Stepney. I did not "take the charge of the operations out of the hands of the executive officers". I did not interfere in any way with the dispositions made by the police authorities on the spot. I never overruled those authorities nor overrode them. From beginning to end the police had an absolutely free hand. I did not hear of the disorders until eleven o'clock, half-an-hour after the Scots Guards had actually reached the scene and begun to fire. I did not send for the Artillery or the Engineers. I was not consulted as to whether they should be sent for.[7] An officer of the Fire Brigade, when forbidden by the police to approach the burning building while shooting was going on, applied personally to me to know if this order had my approval, and I said it had. For the rest, I can claim no more personal responsibility than I can for the sensational accounts which appeared in the newspapers or the spiteful comments based upon them.

> Yours faithfully,
> Winston S. Churchill

11th January

Poland's rejoinder on Saturday was incredulous: was the Home Secretary not in constant touch with the police authorities in Sidney Street during his three-hour visit, and did he never require explanations from them? Having a general responsibility for the actions of the Metropolitan Police, how could he possibly have been present as "a mere casual and interested sightseer"? There must be an immediate inquiry, particularly as Mr Churchill disclaimed responsibility for what was done and placed it entirely on the police.

In its leader the morning after the battle, *The Times* had taken Churchill's implication in the decision-making for granted: "The Home Secretary was present, and the proceedings must have had his authority." On Monday it carried a short letter from Edward Marsh denying that Churchill had called for any explanations from the police and repeating that his responsibility for troops being sent for had been limited to the retrospective sanction—"not legally indispensable"—covering the first party of Scots Guards. This disclaimer implied no censure of police

---

[7] No record seems to exist of how these reinforcements, or the second party of Scots Guards with its machine-gun, came to be sent. Probably they resulted from Major Wodehouse's visit to the War Office.

actions, Marsh added. His final paragraph administered the *coup de grâce*: "Sir Harry Poland has now criticized Mr Churchill, first for interfering with the police, secondly for not interfering with them; and your readers will now wait with interest to see what third position he will take up." But Sir Harry decided to hold his peace.

The same day's *Times* also contained a final letter from Sir West, who welcomed such an emphatic denial of the hitherto uncorrected stories about the Home Secretary's interference in the conduct of the siege; in particular, it now seemed that Churchill did not take the unorthodox view of his duties and powers that many had feared. Nevertheless, his presence must surely have embarrassed those in charge, and had he not approved of their orders, no doubt "unconstitutional interference by a non-expert with the officer in command" would have followed.

Summing up its own opinion of the Home Secretary's attendance in a leader the morning after the inquest on the two dead men had been concluded, *The Times* sided unequivocally with the critics:

> . . . the presence of a high officer of State, who is the official superior of the police, is not desirable on such occasions, and especially in such a conspicuous fashion. It must either embarrass them or prejudge his own proper functions. If he takes command, he interferes with them and paralyses their initiative. If he does not interfere, he tacitly endorses their action. . . . Criticism of them becomes criticism of him, and, since he is a Cabinet Minister, it is at once made a party question. That is not desirable in the public interest.

Churchill's attendance led to much other unflattering comment in the British Press, but a number of people—several of them clearly fellow-Liberals—wrote endorsing his action. Nott-Bower remarked in his memoirs that the Home Secretary's presence gave the policemen concerned in the siege "a feeling of support and of confidence which was highly valued".[8]

Editors were inundated with opinions and suggestions about the conduct of the battle. Comment on the police performance

[8] *Op. cit.*, p. 243.

was mainly uncomplimentary. Why, having evacuated the other occupants, did they retire and leave their quarry the run of the house? Why could they not think beyond pitting bullet against bullet? Nearly all the methods suggested for capturing the fugitives early on were elaborate and impracticable, however; some would also have seriously damaged no. 100. Many favoured the use of fire-hoses or "noxious vapours". A shrewd reader of *Reynolds's Newspaper* claimed that two or three Great Dane police dogs would have overpowered the wanted men in no time, shooting or no shooting. "I recommend Scotland Yard my wall-eyed black beauty," he said.

No official Home Office statement about the battle being forthcoming, rumour and counter-rumour flourished. Reports that no. 100 had been fired on Churchill's instructions were categorically denied. The cause of the fire was (and remains) unknown; the general opinion was that the two men had started it, probably in the hope of escaping in the confusion but perhaps simply as a final, all-engulfing act of destruction.[9]

Random statements by unnamed police officials scarcely helped to clarify matters. Both dead men would have been duly convicted of murder if captured, it was confidently claimed; nevertheless, police opinions about 'Yoshka's' true identity differed, and conflicting views were expressed on other important questions.

Making inquiries at Scotland Yard on 6th January, *The Times* was told that the two dead men "were undoubtedly not Anarchists"; and the next day a "high Metropolitan Police official" put forward an entirely new theory which can have gladdened no hearts at Old Jewry. It was possible, he said, that the deceased had had nothing whatever to do with Exchange Buildings; they might simply have been two foreign Anarchists who thought the police had come to arrest them for crimes committed abroad.

---

[9] According to the Fleischmanns' evidence to the Compensation Board, their stockroom had contained cloth costing £201.19s.10d, some of it made up; amongst the completed garments were twenty-three motor-coats and sixty costumes. It also had in it a gas stove, a sofa, a dining-table, a wringer and probably an accumulation of business papers. There can be little doubt that the fire originated in this room.

The police naturally resented the common misrepresentation of the battle as a straight fight between two villains and a thousand policemen and Guardsmen. It was pointed out that only about fifty of the policemen present had in fact been armed, and not more than twenty of these had participated in the frontal attack on no. 100.

Despite indications to the contrary, the Home Office was not inactive. Immediate consultations on further measures against "armed ruffianism" were arranged. Proposals that the police too should carry arms had been defeated; it was thought preferable to disarm the criminal. In particular, both London Commissioners were strongly opposed to any general arming. *The Times* defined the more effective weapon sought for policemen on dangerous assignments as "a simple, portable arm with considerable stopping-power, rapidity of fire, freedom from recoil and accuracy at a relatively short range. It is primarily for the purpose of defence and not of attack. Some of the most talked-of automatic pistols have a very long range, but the projectile is of small bore and cannot be relied upon to stop a man at close quarters".

On 12th January about a dozen modern makes of pistol were tested on the miniature rifle-range of the 24th Battalion, London Territorial Regiment in Kennington. The Home Secretary, Commissioner Sir Edward Henry, Major Wodehouse and newly appointed Home Office gun-expert Robert Churchill were amongst those present. Winston Churchill played a leading part in the trials, firing several of the pistols and showing a particular interest in the Mauser.[10]

The Metropolitan Police did not receive approval for the purchase of a thousand Webley & Scott automatic pistols until August.[11] The new weapon, for both uniformed and CID branches, was described by the *Standard*:

[10] Churchill could hardly have been totally unfamiliar with the Mauser's performance as he had possessed one for a time during the Boer War.

[11] "This has dragged interminably. Please report when the police are actually to be armed with the pistol," Churchill wrote on the Home Office file on 26th August. (H.O. 45/187326/10595.)

[It] holds nine cartridges, namely eight in the magazine and one in the firing-chamber, the magazine-loading taking place in the handle. Measuring 6¼ inches, the pistol weighs 20 ounces unloaded, while the magazine weighs an additional 2 ounces. The weapon is of ·32 calibre (7·65mm) and discharges automatically a 75-grain bullet at a muzzle velocity of 1,050 feet per second, thus giving it a large potential range, although the point-blank range is only about 20–50 yards.

One consequence of the battle at least was immediate and indisputable. James Charles Buckingham, a seventy-four-year-old ex-Metropolitan police constable, left his Mile End home in the morning of 3rd January and came back trembling with excitement and vexation. "The Houndsditch assassins are killing more policemen," he told his wife. He put the newspaper he was carrying on a table and sat down. "It is awful," he exclaimed. He then threw up his arms and fell back dead. The jury's verdict the next day was death from heart-failure due to excitement.

19. Justification in Law

At 9.50 a.m. on Friday, 6th January, Wynne E. Baxter took his seat in the Stepney coroner's court in Horseferry Branch Road, and ten minutes later the inquest on "the charred remains of two persons at present unknown" had begun. As was then obligatory, the jury of Stepney tradesmen first viewed the corpses. The tiny courtroom was almost exclusively occupied by counsel, who included Archibald Bodkin, policemen and firemen.

Following Baxter's opening remarks, Bodkin explained that he was present on the DPP's instruction to assist the court. The employment of the military in Sidney Street had had every justification in law, he argued. The police were the civil power and had ample authority·to arrest anyone they suspected of being concerned in the Exchange Buildings crimes. Met with violent, armed resistance, they were entitled to overcome it by "any amount of superior force". It having become necessary to enlist the aid of the military because of their superior weapons and proficiency, the military were under the same obligation as other citizens to act in support of the civil power.

Forestalling possible criticism that the pebble-throwing had merely served to confront two aliens with a group of apparent civilians, Bodkin obtained Superintendent Mulvaney's agreement that the uniformed men in the cordons must also have been visible to them. It became apparent when Station Officer Clarke and Fireman Gander testified that a strange twist of fate had reunited the desperate pair in death. From the almost total absence of debris below the second corpse found, Gander thought this man had died where he lay; Clarke took the view that the first body—and much of the debris underneath it—must have fallen into the same room from above.

The divisional police surgeon had performed post-mortems the previous morning. The gist of Dr Grant's evidence follows:

> Body no. 1 appeared to be that of a small man; its measurements seemed to be about 5 inches less than mine, and I am 5 feet 10 inches. Calculations were difficult as both legs were amputated at about the upper third of the thigh, the left arm at the upper third, and the right arm at the lower third. The top of the skull was missing, but about two-thirds of it, including the face, remained.
>
> There was a hole, which I believe to be a bullet-hole, in the occipital bone behind the right ear. This hole went through what was left of the brain, and the bullet had come out at the other side, taking a portion of the skull with it. There was haemorrhage of the brain, and I believe it was this injury that caused death. The injury was far back in the head, and the entrance and exit wounds were on the same level, from which I deduce that it was not self-inflicted.
>
> The heart, liver and kidneys were all quite normal. The stomach was empty. The lungs were charred but healthy and unpigmented, suggesting that their owner was not a city-dweller. All the organs were those of a young adult, probably between twenty and thirty years of age. Such teeth as were found were in good condition.
>
> Body no. 2 had been largely destroyed by fire. Around the neck were the remains of two shirts and two waistcoats. The neck measurement was 16½ inches; the shirts seemed to be of Oxford shirting and the waistcoats of blue serge. The heart, very much

> shrivelled by heat, was that of a young adult; the other organs were
> so destroyed by fire as to make their examination futile. So far as I
> could judge, this man's measurements much resembled the other
> man's. I found no injuries to what remained of the head. The signs
> suggested death by suffocation.

It had not proved possible to match up the skull-cap and other towel contents positively with either body, Dr Grant continued. From his post-mortem examinations and the firemen's evidence, coupled with the facts of the fire in no. 100 travelling downwards and the final shots coming from the ground floor, it was his considered opinion that body no. 1 died first, in an upper room but before being reached by the flames, and that body no. 2 died where it was found.

When the court reassembled on Monday, 9th January, Inspector Wensley was taken through his story and Charles Martin called. He had had Martin's Mansions built; the Fleischmanns were the weekly tenants of no. 100 and could sub-let without reference to him. He wished to make a statement:

Mr Alfred Robinson (witness's solicitor): "I shall ask him a question. Mr Martin, have there been persistent statements in the East End that you or your agent published, or in any way gave notice, that no Englishman need apply for any house on your property?"—"Yes, sir."

"Is it true in any degree?"—"No, sir."

"Has such a notice, either with or without your consent, been put up?"—"Never."[1]

Betsy Gershon alone could provide first-hand evidence as to the identity of one of the two men whose deaths the authorities had brought about. Baxter announced that she was not in custody and showed her a deference which Trassjonsky and Milstein would have envied. Her examination was mainly in English. The substance of her evidence follows:

> My husband, Isaac Gershon, and I came to England from the Crimea
> 5½ years ago. He returned to Yalta eighteen months ago. He was

---

[1] Giving evidence before the Royal Commission on Alien Immigration, a George Brown of Stepney alleged that a letting-bill displayed on a board at Martin's Mansions had included the remark "No English need apply." (Evidence heard by the Commission, 1902–3: Vol. II, p. 87.)

employed as a cap-maker in London but is working as a silver-plater there. He writes to me every week or two. He does not send me money; sometimes I send him some.

Since he left, one man friend and one only has visited me.[2] His name was Josef; I do not know his surname or where he lived. He was a close friend of my husband, who introduced him to me about two years ago. I never saw Josef except at my own house. He came to see me every week or two, but prior to his visit on the Sunday evening he had not called for five or six weeks, when he told me he had some business to attend to in Paris. I do not know whether he actually went. I never had a photograph of him.

Mrs Fleischmann never complained about my having men upstairs. The street door of no. 100 was locked at night by Mr Fleischmann, sometimes at about twelve o'clock and sometimes later.

When Betsy got to know Josef, he and her husband worked at Schneider's, an East End firm of cap-makers. Of Josef and his friend's second visit the evening before the siege, Betsy said:

> I left my work[3] at eight o'clock and went first to a photograph-frame makers, then to see a girl I know. She walked to Sidney Street with me. I arrived back at no. 100 at ten o'clock. The two men came about half an hour later. The street door is sometimes wide open. They came straight upstairs to my room. I was not expecting them. There was a general conversation. Josef spoke Russian, and the other man Lettish. As he also spoke good Yiddish, we talked to each other in that. I did not know him at all and do not know where he lived.
>
> They asked for tea, which I gave them. I went out and bought bread and butter for them and for my own breakfast. I asked Josef why he had come on Sunday and again on Monday; he replied that he had come to say goodbye as he was leaving next morning on a ship. I asked him where he was going, and he said he might go to see his parents. I understood him to mean Russia.
>
> At about midnight—it might have been later, I have no clock or watch—I told them to go home. One of them then said "I won't go home." I said to him, "You must go home," and he answered, "No, it can't be done tonight." Josef said he lived a long way off and could not go.

[2] Betsy tried hard both in court and with the Compensation Board to preserve her respectability.

[3] Betsy was employed at 37 Sidney Street and later at no. 71. Her regular wage for a week of nearly sixty hours was £2.10s.

Baxter was obviously curious to know how so much ammunition had been brought into the house:

> Josef had with him a small brown-paper parcel done up with string. He put it down on the table beside where he sat. He did not open it in my presence. I did not touch it and cannot say how heavy it was. The other man was not carrying anything.
>
> Both wore dark motor-coats with belts at the back, which [Betsy agreed] might have had large inside pockets. The second man looked "altogether wider" than Josef. They did not take their coats off. Neither had ever left anything with me previously.

When she was turned out of her room, Betsy said, she was bewildered and frightened. She sat on the sofa in the stockroom. She could not sleep. No sound came from her own room. After "about an hour" she heard Mrs Fleischmann coming upstairs.

She gave these descriptions of her two visitors:

> Josef was about half a head taller than the other man. He was about twenty-six when I first knew him. He used to have a moustache but on Sunday and Monday was not wearing one. He had a long face, with a thin, straight nose and a dark skin. He was of medium build. In walking he seemed to use his left leg more than the other and give a slight twist to his body.
>
> The other man was somewhere between twenty-three and thirty years old. He was thickset and broad-shouldered, with fair hair, a fair complexion and a broad face.

Next to testify was Rebecca Fleischmann. She had seen Betsy go up to her room by herself late in the evening before the siege. She had not seen anyone else go up. She herself went to bed about midnight after bolting the front door.

On Sunday afternoon, the day before this sitting, a Belgian Browning automatic had been discovered in the debris behind no. 100. This was now produced, Superintendent Ottaway remarking that one such weapon had been used in Exchange Buildings and another found amongst Morountzeff's effects at 44 Gold Street.

Guided by Bodkin, Chief Superintendent Stark and Superintendent Mulvaney outlined the events of 2nd and 3rd January and explained the decisions reached. The court considered the circumstances in which the firemen had been obliged to stand

and watch no. 100 burn. Sergeant Thurlow told of the last shots fired from the back of the house after the firemen had begun work at the front. It became clear that the firemen's grievance was not to be lightly abandoned. Led by Baxter, Station Officer Edmonds gave evidence about his application to Churchill:

"You were informed that the Home Secretary was present and in charge of the operations?"—"Yes."

"Did you go to the Home Secretary?"—"Yes . . . I told him I represented the brigade and wanted instructions."

Edmonds was explicit at first that he had been told by Churchill personally that he could not do anything; later, however, he conceded that it might have been somebody with him. On Bodkin's intervention, Stark was recalled to testify that he had been standing beside the Home Secretary when Edmonds came up; the station officer had addressed Churchill, but he, Stark, had given him his answer.[4] Edmonds admitted that, when he heard about the shooting from no. 100, he felt it would be "discreet" not to advance. To pour water effectively into a room, a fireman would have to be opposite it at a suitable height and within about 70 feet.

When Assistant Divisional Officer Morris also began to talk about the Home Secretary's instructions, Bodkin's calm deserted him. No one in the police wanted to escape responsibility for preventing the firemen from being killed, he declared in exasperation. By the time the court reassembled on 18th January, Churchill had decided to enter the witness-box himself.

Bodkin's first task was to reinforce the slender evidence of identity. Detective Sergeant Weston deposed that on Sunday, 8th January, he had come across two keys amongst the debris in no. 100. He showed these, with others he had found, to the landladies of 59 Grove Street and 44 Gold Street; Lizzie Katz identified one key as having been handed to one of her two former lodgers, and Polly Kempler said the other was Morountzeff's. Each key opened the appropriate street door;[5] one had been lying near each body.

---

[4] Churchill's letter to *The Times*, in which he admitted having spoken to Edmonds, appeared three days after the station officer's evidence was given.

[5] The front-door locks on such houses were of a cheap standard type; it might have been illuminating to know how many others the two keys also fitted.

Dr Grant was recalled to state that he had removed what remained of the right thigh-bone from body no. 1 and found evidence of an old fracture. This would probably have caused some shortening and thus a limp. Further examinations showed that no. 1 was the taller man, though probably not more than 5 feet 6 inches. Asked by Baxter if he could have been 6 feet, the doctor said he thought that quite impossible.

Sergeant Thurlow was recalled to describe his warning to the firemen behind no. 100 and the delay that resulted, also his earlier glimpse of the two besieged. Stark was recalled and questioned by J. W. Godfrey, the LCC's solicitor: as a City policeman, had he any authority to give directions to the Metropolitan Fire-Brigade? Stark thought he had in the circumstances. The LCC had a statutory duty to perform through its fire-brigade, Godfrey explained, and someone had prevented this. He wanted the responsibility placed on that person. Stark was emphatic that the sole reason for the order had been to save firemen's lives.

Coming quickly to the rescue, Bodkin established that Stark and Superintendent Mulvaney had acted in concert, each stopping some of the firemen. Recalled once more, Mulvaney said he had held them up at the Whitechapel Road end of Sidney Street. Nobody had instructed him to.

Churchill, the last witness, gave evidence for twenty minutes. If his story, as tactfully elicited by Bodkin, rationalized his actions more than it helped the court, he told it with a disarming candour. In addition to the reasons already recorded, he had been present in Sidney Street "to support [the police] if necessary in any unusual difficulty in which they might require some authority".[6]

To prevent the firemen from risking their lives by attempting to deal with the fire at once was the only possible course to which anybody could have consented, Churchill declared.[7] Of

[6] These explanations were dismissed without ceremony in next morning's *Times* leader already referred to. They did nothing, the writer remarked acidly, to remove the general feeling that he committed an error of judgment in being present.

[7] Writing to the Prime Minister on the day of the battle, Churchill put his attitude more trenchantly: "I thought it better to let the house burn down rather than spend good British lives in rescuing those ferocious rascals." Randolph S.

Edmonds's approach to him he said: "He came up to me where I was standing and said that the fire-brigade had arrived and that he understood he was not to put out the fire at present. 'Was this all right?' Or words to that effect. I said 'Quite right; I accept full responsibility.' I wish to make it clear that these words referred to the specific question asked me and that I confirmed and supported the police in their action."

After touching on Churchill's subsequent conversation with Morris, Bodkin fed him several convenient questions. Churchill largely repeated the denials in his letter to *The Times*. He wanted to place on record, he said, the "general and perfect readiness" of the police to volunteer for a rush on no. 100 at any time. When he remarked that he thought the firemen had acted very properly in making sure they had "the highest covering authority" for watching the house burn, Godfrey intervened to establish that by this he meant the highest covering police authority—himself.

Baxter's address to the jury fully endorsed the course taken against the two besieged. Speaking of the legal position of the police when their quarry opened fire and Sergeant Leeson was wounded, he referred to Sir Matthew Hale's time-honoured dictum and paraphrased current authorities on the subject: "When officers of justice are resisted in the legal execution of their duty, they may repel force by force, and if in so doing they kill the party or parties resisting them, it is justifiable homicide; and the same rule applies to persons acting in their aid." The military had been called in not as soldiers but as armed civilians, said Baxter, and he quoted an army regulation authorizing their use in such a situation on the initiative of an army officer alone.[8] He thought the two men's conduct "impossible of explanation except as an ample admission of their guilt of a capital crime, the despair of desperate men without hope".

The jury took half an hour to decide that body no. 1 was that of the man known as Josef and body no. 2 that of the man known as Fritz. They considered that Josef's death had been caused by a

Churchill, *Winston S. Churchill*: Companion Volume II (Heinemann, 1969), p. 1033.

[8] King's Regulations and Orders for the Army (1908), Reg. 967.

shot wound inflicted by an unknown soldier and was a case of justifiable homicide, and that Fritz died from suffocation. They added a rider expressing their hope for more stringent laws regarding criminal aliens entering the United Kingdom.

20. The Hot Fit and the Cold Fit

Although overshadowed by other controversial actions of his, particularly his handling of the disorders in South Wales the previous autumn, Churchill's part in the Battle of Stepney did not pass unremarked in the House of Commons. The first derogatory comments of any consequence came from the Leader of the Opposition, A. J. Balfour, on 6th February, during the debate on the Address to the new Parliament.

Churchill was lounging at the Prime Minister's side, his hands thrust deep into his pockets, as Balfour spoke. The Home Office was not usually "a perpetual source of interest and surprise to friends and critics", Balfour remarked banteringly, "but much turns upon the personality of the holder of the office". He gathered that the Home Secretary, although present among the huge forces assembled in Sidney Street, had had nothing at all to do with them being there:

> He was there in—well, I do not know the position he was in. He was, I understand, in military phrase, in what is known as the zone of fire—he and a photographer were both risking valuable lives. I understand what the photographer was doing, but what was the right honourable gentleman doing? That I neither understood at the time, nor do I understand now. I must frankly say that I should have thought that anything more embarrassing to those responsible for the operations than to have the head of the office who is over them all present with the photographer as irresponsible spectators, could not be imagined. I cannot imagine anything more embarrassing to those who had to carry out what evidently, from the result, must have been a very difficult and dangerous military operation.

Balfour had also, in more serious vein, criticized Churchill's conduct of affairs in South Wales. "I believe," the Prime Minister said in reply to this, "that my right honourable friend . . . will be shown to have exercised from first to last a wise discretion." On Churchill's connections with Sidney Street, Asquith was not to be drawn. His right honourable friend suffered from "the dangerous endowment of an interesting personality", he said lightly; photographers sought his company because they knew he interested the general public.

However, the prolonged vilification of the Aliens Act and its administration which had taken place during past weeks had made the general question of alien immigration far too prominent to be so easily disposed of. One Unionist member's amendment to the Address on the subject was nullified when another, Edward Goulding, announced that he would introduce a Bill.

Churchill himself had seen quite clearly the wisdom of bending with the wind as far as the strong Radical sentiments on his side of the House would allow. "I think I shall have to stiffen the administration and the Aliens Act a little," he wrote to Asquith on 3rd January, the day of the siege, "and more effective measures must be taken by the police to supervise the dangerous classes of alien in our midst." No doubt his resolve was reinforced by a letter which one of George V's private secretaries sent him two days later, giving him the King's view: "He hopes that these outrages by foreigners will lead you to consider whether the Aliens Act could not be amended so as to prevent London from being infested with men and women whose presence would not be tolerated in any other country." Churchill's reply included details of ideas he had for new legislation.

On 19th January his fellow Cabinet members received from him a draft Bill accompanied by a memorandum remarking that "Two naughty principles are involved . . . a deliberate differentiation between the alien, and especially the unassimilated alien, and a British subject, and . . . that an alien may, in certain circumstances, be deported before he has committed an offence."[1]

---

[1] This quotation and the preceding one are from Randolph S. Churchill, *Winston S. Churchill*: Volume II, *Young Statesman, 1901–14* (Heinemann, 1966), pp. 410,

Exchange Buildings and Sidney Street thus set two Bills in motion. The Private Member's Bill, a hastily conceived measure seeking to strengthen and extend the Aliens Act as a whole, had an uneventful first reading on 9th February; Churchill announced that his Government Bill was also in the offing.

Numerous critics of the Act wanted alien immigrants to be obliged to register with the police, as Britons had to do on the Continent. Goulding's amending Bill laid down that every alien immigrant travelling steerage to permanent residence in the United Kingdom must do so. It made it an offence for aliens to possess or carry a pistol without a permit from the police or a court, and wide powers of arrest and search were given. Amongst other things, the Bill also required undertakings from their prospective employers that alien immigrants would be paid fair wages as prescribed by law.[2]

Within its narrower limits, the Home Secretary's Aliens (Prevention of Crime) Bill was in several respects a more severe measure than Goulding's. On a complaint to a court, an alien with suspected criminal tendencies who had not lived in Britain for the previous five years (or had been convicted of a serious offence during that time) could be required—under pain of expulsion—to enter into recognizances and provide sureties as to his future behaviour. The provisions regarding aliens possessing pistols resembled those in the other Bill.

The unsatisfactory situation regarding expulsion (generally known as deportation) under the Act had drawn particularly forceful comment. Churchill's Bill inverted the procedure: instead of only recommending the expulsion of an alien convicted of a serious offence when they chose to, the courts would advise the Home Secretary of every such conviction and state their reasons if expulsion was *not* recommended.

411. The extract from Churchill's letter to Asquith is from Companion Volume II of the same work, p. 1033.

[2] The London Committee of Deputies of British Jews took strong exception to this fair wages clause, arguing that "The work of a raw alien . . . cannot be expected to command the rates of wages referred to." The Home Office file bears the laconic comment: "Their remarks . . . rather give away the practice of sweating the alien 'greener' and indeed all employees in the trades where he undercuts wages." (H.O.45/206332/10641.)

Churchill did not introduce his Bill until 18th April. Mindful of the delicate ground which many would consider him to be treading, his manner was (to quote *The Times*) "subdued and apologetic". This Bill did not touch alien immigration, he pointed out, and dealt only with alien crime. It would not be practicable, nor "worth the money and the vexation", to attempt to keep undesirables out by placing under immigration law all the eighty or ninety ports where aliens were liable to land;[3] he was also sure that registration of aliens was unnecessary and would be neither convenient nor desirable.

Speaking of his proposal to invert the courts' expulsion procedure, Churchill turned the tables neatly on some of the harshest critics. In general, the courts had been failing to take advantage of their expulsion powers under the Aliens Act, he said, and investigation often showed the very magistrates and recorders who had recently made scathing speeches about its lax administration to have been responsible. Less than a fifth of the convicted aliens received into prison in 1910 had been recommended for expulsion.

Regarding the provision about sureties, Churchill explained that the Government was resolute to avoid two things: withdrawal of the right of asylum and any unnecessary disturbance of the great bulk of the country's alien population, mainly Jewish, which was in overwhelming degree peaceful, hard-working and law-abiding. The person they wished to deal with was the unassimilated alien:

> The man whom we have in mind in this provision is the man of whom we know nothing and who knows nothing of us or of our institutions and peaceful life, who comes from a country where murder and violence are common, where every policeman is regarded as a foe, where every institution is regarded as tyranny and where to carry on a career of plunder and rapine like a fierce wild animal may be deemed to be a romantic and even a respectable profession.

[3] The Aliens Act was only operated at thirteen major ports. As long as the "twenty or less" ships remained exempt from its provisions, the fact that many of them landed their passengers elsewhere was immaterial; but Goulding's Bill withdrew their exemption.

The Government also intended shortly to introduce a Pistols Bill in the House of Lords, Churchill said. His remark that the present Bill would empower the police, "if they have reason to believe that an alien is carrying a pistol, to ask him for his licence, and in default to take his name and address" caused some sardonic laughter. He suggested that his Bill be set down for second reading after Goulding's; a grand committee might then consider both together. It was given its first reading amid cheers.

A meeting of advanced Radical members two days later took exception to the clause requiring sureties on suspicion. The scope this would give to informants, police and courts was considered far too wide.

During February and March, Parliamentary questions about the Aliens Act and alien criminals had been frequent. After December and January's exhilarating newspaper chase,[1] many of the details Churchill supplied came as a distinct anticlimax. Admissions to Britain under the proviso regarding religious and political refugees in the Act itself and Gladstone's benefit-of-the-doubt instruction, upon which so much indignation had been heaped, had totalled less than a hundred over the previous four years. Even in 1906, when the troubles in Eastern Europe were at crisis-point, the number admitted was only 505. The figure for 1910, when 610,776 aliens entered the United Kingdom and 597,506 left, was five.

Goulding's Bill passed its second reading on Friday, 28th April, by a small majority. Radical and Labour opposition to it was intense. His party, Ramsay MacDonald declared in a withering speech, did not agree with "a single line, clause or provision" of the Bill. He expressed particularly strong fears about the powers it gave the detective police:

[1] Some of the statistics published about aliens during this hot pursuit, and the arguments based on them, were grossly misleading. To take one outstanding example, several Tory newspapers printed what purported to be annual figures showing that London's alien population had grown from 41,000 to 136,000 in the four years from 1904 to 1908; these were in fact the ten-yearly census totals for the forty years from 1861 to 1901. Exposing the misrepresentation, the Liberal Press was biting: the *Star* headed its leader 'Faking the Figures'.

> There are two sections of police officers, and we must remember the
> two sections when we deal with this Bill. . . . There is the faithful
> public servant who parades our streets in uniform. We know him
> afar off—we see him going round the corner—there is no doubt
> about him. . . . There is the other gentleman whom you do not
> know; you find him in the middle of your political refugees, acting as
> their friend and their prompter. I think honourable gentlemen
> opposite have heard of 'Peter the Painter'. I think they have heard of
> Father Gapon, and I think they have heard of others in recent years.
> That is the gentleman, and that is the section of the police force, that
> is going to be let loose by clause one [the registration clause] of this
> Bill, and who, once he is let loose, is going to play havoc with the
> right of political asylum in this country.

'Father Gapon's Revolution'—otherwise known as 'Bloody
Sunday' or 'Red Sunday'—occurred in St Petersburg in January
1905. *Agents provocateurs* were understood to have played a
prominent part in the incident, in which workers parading in
front of the Tsar's palace were shot down. MacDonald was
obviously one of those people who saw Peter the Painter as a
Russian Government agent, working to create a state of public
opinion in Britain that would lead to Eastern European revolutionaries being denied asylum and bring sympathy for his
government's policies.

The vehemence of MacDonald's attack particularly displeased
The Times, which worked some savage irony at his and his party's
expense into next morning's leader:

> [Their] pronounced affection for foreigners is perhaps explained by
> their curious inability to understand their own
> countrymen. . . . According to the Socialists, every law for con-
> trolling immigration destroys the right of asylum. . . . Mr Ramsay
> MacDonald and his friends have, as we know, a weakness for
> criminals. . . . But the British people . . . have enough criminals of
> their own, which is not a reason for welcoming foreign ones in
> addition, as Mr MacDonald seems to think, but the contrary.

An aside of MacDonald's boded ill for Churchill's Bill: "The
Government Bill is not before us, or I should have something to
say to it. I am dealing with the Bill of the hour, and the other Bill
will be equally faithfully dealt with should I get the opportunity."
Churchill found himself in general agreement with

MacDonald's views, he told the House. He enlarged on the practical objections to registration and bringing far more of Britain's ports under immigration law. A huge administrative commitment would be involved, yet any criminal alien had only to buy a first-class ticket to avoid the whole paraphernalia. The registration requirement must come out of the Bill, or the Government would oppose it.

The Government's Bill was not reached until after five o'clock and a formal objection to its second reading there and then was successful. Replying to a Radical inquiry about it on Monday, Churchill was vague. Reminded that many members had voted for the second reading of Goulding's Bill only because they thought his Bill would also be going to the grand committee, his reply was enigmatic: "It makes no difference," he said.

Amongst the many letters about the Aliens Act which *The Times* published in January was one from Sir Mackenzie Chalmers, who had been Permanent Under-Secretary at the Home Office from 1903 to 1908 and had chaired the inter-departmental committee which framed the original rules under the Act. His letter remarked that, "The British public, or at any rate the vocal part of it, is always suffering from a hot fit or a cold fit, and it is no use proposing measures during the hot fit which will be execrated and emasculated when the cold fit succeeds."

Four months had now elapsed since the Battle of Stepney. The majority of newspapers and their readers had long since passed on to other things. There were, for instance, reports of young English girls being recruited by the Mormons, shipped to the United States and seduced into polygamous relationships; these naturally aroused intense interest and indignation. However, whilst the hot fit about alien immigration had given way to the cold outside Parliament, and even to an appreciable extent on the Opposition benches, Radical and Labour convictions remained. The odds against any new (and reasonably efficacious) legislation had lengthened still further.

They were not accepted. Pressure of Government business continued to be phenomenally heavy. Parliamentary time was never found for the Aliens (Prevention of Crime) Bill, eventually withdrawn, and Goulding's amending Bill died a natural death on the prorogation of Parliament. The regulations upon which so much controversy had centred remained unrevised until 1915. Exchange Buildings and Sidney Street did, however, lead to various administrative improvements, such as the strengthening of the aliens department at the Home Office, which paid valuable dividends when war came.

The proposed Pistols Bill lingered on. It met considerable opposition from the trade, especially in the Midlands. A useful measure gradually evolved but was still unborn when war broke out in August 1914.

21. Recollection, Restitution and Reward

Following the startling events of 3rd January 1911, Sidney Street became, in the *Daily Chronicle*'s words, "a sort of Mecca of the curious". Not until 5.10 the next afternoon, by which time a hoarding enclosing the front of no. 100 had been completed, were the cordons withdrawn and the immense crowds allowed to pass slowly up and down in the darkness. The previous day, local children had admired the artillerymen's horses and equipment; now it was the turn of the liveried chauffeurs in shiny motor-cars bringing men and women of substance from the West End. A long line of taxi-cabs outside Aldgate Station quickly became a familiar sight. Controlled by a large body of foot and mounted police, the sightseers' pilgrimage continued for over a week.

The smashed panes, split window-frames and innumerable jagged white bullet-scars across the road were examined almost as intently as what could still be seen of the desolate, roofless shell of no. 100, also heavily pock-marked, with its blackened interior and dripping cistern still attached to an upper wall. The atmosphere resembled that of a lying-in-state. Battle of Stepney picture-postcards, mostly showing Churchill at the scene surrounded by policemen, sold extremely well, and there was a brisk trade in flattened bullets and other souvenirs.

Amongst the important people escorted by Superintendent Mulvaney and his officers on tours of the battlefield were the Chancellor of the Exchequer, Lloyd George, and the Attorney General, Sir Rufus Isaacs. The speculation and false rumours continued. Nothing seemed too improbable to be believed. Even *The Times* reported on 5th January that "twelve Mauser and several Browning pistols" had been found in the ruined house. Behind the hoarding a meticulous examination of the debris was not completed until 11th January.

Two of the reported discoveries, a woman's wig and some hollow metal cylinders with slightly tapered ends, provoked eager comment. The *Daily Telegraph* was convinced the latter were bomb-cases. "A day's delay in laying siege to the Anarchists' hiding-place," it asserted, "might have enabled the two criminals to obtain the powerful explosives with which to charge the cases." Next day, however, these mysterious objects were revealed to be accessories for the Fleischmanns' button-cutting machine.

The wig intrigued many people who brushed aside categorical police statements that the siege and Leon Beron's murder were completely unconnected. A mysterious broadly built woman was supposed to have figured in the Clapham Common case, and if, as some keen amateur criminologists thought, this person was really a man in disguise, he could well have been wearing just such a wig. Here again the explanation proved sadly mundane: it belonged to old Mrs Clements, who still affected the *shartel*.[1] The irony of a stream of lead (probably a melted roof-flashing) drenching Fritz Svaars's body after so many purposeful bullets had apparently missed it passed unnoticed.

Newsmen kept Rebecca Fleischmann's alert imagination, overworked memory and ready tongue constantly busy. At four o'clock on the afternoon of the siege an enterprising reporter carried her off, still only half-dressed, from 102 Sidney Street to

---

[1] Continental rabbis of old considered it immoral for a married woman to wear her hair loose, and an ancient Jewish ordinance required her to have it shorn. She then covered her head with a kerchief or, in more modern times, the wig (*shartel*).

his house in Kensington. Rebecca rewarded him with her longest and most detailed Press statement, which the *Daily Telegraph* printed on 5th January.

Relations between Betsy Gershon and the Fleischmanns had been guarded. The Gershons had a two-year-old son whom Betsy now boarded out in Barnsbury. Since her husband's return to their homeland with appendicitis, her life had been an uneventful one centred on the boy, her work and the Russian books she was forever reading; though amiable enough, she showed little desire for company. The Fleischmanns were somewhat in awe of her, considering her well educated and suspecting her of Anarchist views. Rebecca was convinced she had deliberately avoided discussing the Exchange Buildings murders.

A remark of Betsy's twelve months before the siege sprang to Rebecca's mind. Samuel had asked their lodger point-blank one day whether she believed in God. "There's no God," Betsy told him shortly. "I laugh at all them things." From that moment, Rebecca said, she ceased to like the other woman. Communication between family and lodger became more reserved. The Fleischmanns' elder daughter, who made underclothes at Gardiner's (a well-known Whitechapel store) and who often visited Betsy's room in the evenings to help her with extra sewing-work, was discouraged from doing so, and Rebecca's natural inquisitiveness became more closely concerned with Betsy's behaviour. The contemptuous remark also rankled with Samuel, a God-fearing Jew who (as he put it) kept his religion; the two had frequent minor disputes afterwards.

Rebecca recounted several happenings during the week-end before the siege; none of these, however, demonstrated more than her deep distrust of the other woman, whom she now—reasonably enough—held responsible for the subsequent catastrophe.

Betsy normally kept her room locked in her absence. Rebecca cleaned the second-floor stairs and passage on alternate Fridays and, doing so as usual on 30th December, had been surprised not to see daylight through Betsy's keyhole. Betsy was of course out at work. Rebecca could not remember the keyhole ever having been dark before and concluded that the door must be locked with the key on the inside, but Samuel suggested that Betsy had probably hung a dress or coat inside the door.

That same evening, Rebecca added, while Betsy was still out, she crossed the street and looked up at her window. It was dark. She also thought that, later that night, she had seen her lodger push someone out of the front door. "Who is that?" she had called. "Oh, Mrs Fleischmann," Betsy replied, "it's only me."

Samuel's traveller came in between 9 a.m. and 9.30 nearly every day, including Saturdays. Rebecca went upstairs at about 8.30 next morning to light the gas-stove in the stockroom and at once smelled cigarette-smoke in the second-floor passage and on the attic stairs. Betsy, Rebecca and Davis Schiemann were all non-smokers, and Samuel had given up smoking on the Sabbath since his father's death some months before; the traveller smoked but had not come in yet. Her suspicions instantly reawakened, Rebecca sought Samuel out and told him. Samuel was unimpressed and forgot all about the incident.

On the Sunday morning, Rebecca said, Davis Schiemann told her that his nine-year-old daughter had surprised a thief, a young man of about twenty, in his room. Rebecca had tried several times during the week-end to get her husband or one of their sons into Betsy's room on various pretexts. Unfortunately, Samuel's half-hearted co-operation proved unequal to the occasion, and Betsy told the boy to wait outside.

Betsy had shown herself to be a smooth liar, and there was much scepticism about her story of the wanted men's two visits; in particular, several police officers scorned her assertion that their second appearance had not been until about 10.30 on Monday night, by which time no. 100 was supposedly under close surveillance. This was "an obvious lie", Nott-Bower wrote.[2] Many people were tempted to believe—as Rebecca obviously did—that she had in fact been sheltering them for some time.

But to infer their presence from the story of Schiemann's intruder presupposed that they would be foolhardy enough to wander round no. 100 in broad daylight. This was unthinkable. In addition, Betsy later told the Compensation Board that she had

---

[2] *Op. cit.*, p. 240.

entertained other company "that was in my place all Sunday". The fugitives could not possibly have been concealed in her room at the same time. Nor would the stockroom or workroom have been safe hiding-places, except possibly at night; the Fleischmanns and Samuel's half-dozen employees were in and out of both far too frequently.

Betsy always returned to no. 100 for her midday meal, and Rebecca remembered another visitor to her room at 2.15 on Monday afternoon, the day before the battle. This was a fair, long-haired and rather shabbily dressed man who carried under his arm something long and slender covered in American cloth. Betsy called to Rebecca over the banisters that he had come to take her photograph. He left shortly before three o'clock, and she went back to work.[3]

The Compensation Board asked Betsy the question already put to her at the inquest: how did she think the two men had got into the house on Monday night? "I suppose they knocked at the door," she said this time, "or the door was open." Two desperate men, one with a price on his head, were unlikely to knock politely for admission, but Sidney Street was ill-lit and far from deserted in the late evening, and no. 100's front door opened onto the pavement. As it was often left open, they could have slipped through it and up the stairs one at a time easily enough. The fact that both Rebecca and Samuel were out, separately, for some time between about nine o'clock and midnight reinforced this explanation. They could well have got in the same way on Sunday.

Rebecca remembered Josef calling on Betsy two or three times during the previous summer. She described him as a tall, dark man with big moustaches and curly hair at the side of his head. Inquisitive as ever, Rebecca went up to Betsy's room one evening when he was there; Josef was sitting quietly reading a Russian newspaper. She heard Betsy let him out at about midnight. Soon

---

[3] In *The Houndsditch Murders and the Siege of Sidney Street* (Macmillan, 1973), Donald Rumbelow wrote that, according to some pencilled notes in surviving City Police files, this Monday afternoon visitor must have been the informant who put the police on to 100 Sidney Street. Having thus led them to Fritz Svaars, he was later paid a third of the £500 reward; his identity, however, remains unknown.

after his first call, her curiosity overcame her: "You will excuse me, Mrs Gershon, who is the gentleman?" He was her husband's cousin, Betsy said. Rebecca had not seen him since about August.

The battle was a cruel calamity for both no. 100's families. Mrs Schiemann and her two infants were taken in by one neighbour, the other two children by a second, and Schiemann himself by a third. The Fleischmanns had lost not only their home but the premises, machinery,[4] stock and records of Samuel's eighteen-year-old business; Samuel was reduced to buying a jacket from Blustein at no. 102. Applying on 10th January for enforcement of a debt-repayment order, he could not produce the plaint note; the court was sympathetic and supplied him with a substitute.

Neither Fleischmann nor Schiemann was insured. That the two families (and others less pressingly affected) had a moral right to redress was generally admitted, but the situation was quite unprecedented, and none of the authorities concerned would accept responsibility for it. No grounds existed for argument that the police or the military had exceeded their powers in any way. A disturbance not constituting a riot unless at least three persons took part in it, the Riot (Damages) Act of 1886 could not be invoked. Claims were received by the Government, the LCC, the Metropolitan Police and several other bodies. Samuel's solicitor promptly lodged one at Guildhall; the City Solicitor replied equally swiftly repudiating all liability.

Charles Martin, whose ten houses—Martin's Mansions, 1 Hawkins Street and 2 Lindley Street—had been insured for £6,000, fared no better. The insurance company took the view that his loss had arisen from civil commotion. They would have met his claim, they remarked, had the fire-brigade been allowed to function properly; the outbreak could then have been dealt with in ten minutes and the total loss averted.

Immediately after the siege, however, Martin's main concern was the reappearance of the "no English need apply" story, which he regarded as a personal affront. He had never refused an English applicant, he declared; the fact was that English people

---

[4] This included four Singer sewing-machines, a large button-machine, a small button-machine and a button-cutting machine. The large button-machine, which Rebecca operated, was American and cost £72.

did not care to live as close neighbours with Jews. The offending words had been written in chalk by some unknown person. He attributed the story to spite and envy.

The plight of no. 100's innocent victims was raised in the House of Commons early in March, and later that month Churchill announced that he had appointed two MPs, Sir Henry Dalziel and A. C. Morton, to head a Compensation Board. Morton, who was erstwhile deputy chairman of its police committee, had been nominated by the City Corporation. Such payments as were decided upon would be made "as a matter of grace" from the two police funds in equal shares.[5]

Public money was at stake, and Dalziel and Morton were both Scotsmen. The Board weighed each claim exhaustively for the smallest suggestion of inflation or impropriety. Its knowledge of the complexities of the siege, however, was sometimes sketchy: "But after the shooting ended and the fire commenced," Morton observed plaintively at one point, "no effort was made to save any of this property."

The claims amounted to £2,193.6s in all. At £907.11s.7d, including £48.4s for his wife's jewellery and £250 for loss of business, Samuel's was the largest. The Fleischmanns and the Schiemanns, who claimed £133, were particularly aggrieved about the police refusal to allow them to visit no. 100 during the long hiatus between the evacuation and the first shooting: "Mr Fleischmann's contention all along," Samuel's solicitor told the Board, "has been that he was told over and over again by the police, 'Don't go in; we will see everything is right.'" Chief Superintendent Stark denied that anyone had said their property would be safe.

The Schiemanns' rent had been 7s.6d a week and Betsy's 4s.6d. All no. 100's lodgers had provided their own furniture and furnishings. Betsy calculated her losses at £75.4s.6d. Whatever her political leanings, she believed in some of the orthodoxies; she had owned a set of Russian furs since the previous autumn

---

[5] The Riot (Damages) Act authorized payment of compensation from police funds. It is most unlikely that the Home Office would have required the payments to be made from police sources in this way if it had not been satisfied that the losses and damage had not resulted from political activity.

and at the time of the siege had £43 in the bank. She had heard regularly from her husband until the last few weeks, Betsy told the Board; the London police had been in touch with the Russian police about him, and he was "in trouble".

The Board's tenacious questioning about Josef failed to shake her composure. She had not asked him about his recent employment. She emphatically denied ever having known him to have plenty of money. Had she not suspected that he and his fair-haired companion were doubtful characters? "No," answered Betsy sardonically, "I was not clever enough."

Martin's ten houses had cost about £7,000 to build. He claimed £600, £450 of which was for rebuilding the burnt-out house; the Board considered £300, or perhaps £350, more realistic. Another £80 was for loss of rent; Samuel had paid 34 shillings a week, and the tenants of nos. 98 and 102 had given notice to quit. Other claims included one of £15 from the owner of 103 to 119 Sidney Street across the way.

Having exercised its whittling skills to the limit, the Board recommended payments totalling £533.0s.2d. Martin was awarded £175 towards no. 100's reconstruction, and Davis Schiemann £65. Samuel was allowed less than a third of his claim, and Betsy Gershon nothing. The Receiver of the Metropolitan District made the payments.

Detective Sergeant Leeson's experiences made him a ten-day celebrity. Sympathizers sent him and the hearthstone's victims a profusion of flowers; messages arrived from the King. Both the sergeant's lungs had been severely damaged, and for some days pneumonia or bronchitis was feared. As with Sergeant Woodhams, his recovery was to be slow and difficult; not until 8th February was he considered fit enough to leave the London Hospital's Gloucester Ward for a convalescent home at Felixstowe. The Metropolitan Police upgraded him to first-class sergeant on 10th January, and on 23rd February the newspapers announced a King's Police Medal for him; unhappily, the promotion only preceded his invaliding out, and the story about his decoration proved false.

To a hard-working and conscientious policeman like Benjamin Leeson, these were harsh blows. During his long spell of enforced idleness, the Exchange Buildings–Sidney Street affair preyed increasingly on his mind. He was well enough to be present, closely and nervously attentive, when the Old Bailey trial of Jacob Peters and others took place at the beginning of May. When, on medical advice, he embarked shortly afterwards for Australia, his shipboard companions were soon calling him 'Peter the Painter'; as will be seen later, the case continued to obsess him even on the other side of the world.

The fire-brigade's other casualties were soon back on duty, but District Officer Pearson's injury was infinitely more serious; his spine had been fractured. "Pearson will never move again, except by the aid of his fellows," said the Hon. Harry Lawson, Unionist MP for Mile End. On 31st January the LCC approved his promotion to superintendent.

While Pearson continued to lie in the London Hospital, the Hon. Sydney Holland drew the King's attention to his case, and His Majesty took a close interest in it. The Royal Hospital for Incurables on Putney Heath and the British Home and Hospital for Incurables at Streatham competed for him. On 7th March he was reported to be "an accepted candidate for admission" to the Royal Hospital, but within forty-eight hours it had been outbid; a wealthy lady having founded a memorial bed at the British Home and Hospital and nominated the stricken man, it could accept him immediately. Four months later, on 8th July 1911, Charles Edward Pearson died there.

The charitable appeals arising from Exchange Buildings continued to be handsomely supported. Many *Daily Express* readers ignored the closure of its fund, and by 3rd January it had risen to £1,933.19s.8d. On 21st January, Alderman Sir Marcus Samuel, as chairman of the Portsoken Ward Relief Fund, sent the City Police Commissioner a cheque for £527.10s.11d. On 11th May William Thomas Bryant and Ernest Richard Woodhams were each presented with a gold watch on the Ward's behalf.

"The Corporation," wrote Nott-Bower in his memoirs, "granted pensions on the most generous scale to the widows and children of the murdered men."[6] The description is open to

---

[6] *Op. cit.*, p. 235.

question. By not deciding how it would meet its obligations until long after private charity had produced a princely sum, the City of London much reduced them. The Court of Common Council approved the following grants at the beginning of March: to Mrs Tucker and Mrs Bentley, 30 shillings a week each so long as they remained widows; to Bentley's two children, 5 shillings a week each until they were fifteen; and to Sylvia May Choat, Choat's unmarried sister, 5 shillings a week so long as she remained single.

The provision for the two wounded men, however, gave no grounds for criticism. Woodhams's retirement was announced in mid-February and Bryant's a month later. They were to receive pensions of 42s.6d and 52s.6d a week respectively, the maximum rates for their new ranks.

The Lord Mayor presented the murdered men's medals to Mrs Tucker, Mrs Bentley and one of Choat's brothers at a Mansion House ceremony on 15th March. Bryant and Woodhams had already received theirs at St James's Palace on 23rd February. Woodhams was obliged to attend the investiture on a stretcher and went by motor-ambulance; the waiting crowd, although unable to catch so much as a glimpse of him, cheered him loudly. With His Majesty in the Throne Room were Churchill, who as Home Secretary read out the citations, and the Lord Chamberlain; Woodhams's stretcher was placed in front of the royal dais, and the invalid, wearing the Coronation medal on his new sergeant's uniform, saluted lying on his back.

The Battle of Stepney brought further recognition of services rendered. On 18th February the magistrate at Thames police court presented the three civilians mainly concerned in Leeson's evacuation—Dr Johnstone, Lewis Levy and Frank Gascoyne— with Carnegie Hero Fund awards: a personally inscribed medal and £25 for the doctor, a certificate and £10 each for the other two men. "He serves God best who most nobly serves humanity," the medal said.

On 28th January the Home Secretary had authorized payments to the trio from Metropolitan Police funds: a special 20-guinea fee for Dr Johnstone, a grant of £15 for Levy and another of £5 for Gascoyne, "in consideration of the gallantry displayed by them . . .''. A payment of £12, £10 as a personal fee and £2 for damage, was offered to Dr Solomon Krestin of 98 Sidney Street ''in recognition of his services''; there being no reference to gallantry (or, it will be noticed, to guineas rather than pounds for his professional services), Dr Krestin took offence and turned it down. He had second thoughts later on and accepted the money in August.

On Sunday night, 2nd April 1911, the ten-yearly census took place. Unusual difficulties were experienced with the aliens in Stepney, Mile End and elsewhere, many of whom were sure that the forms must be connected with the Exchange Buildings affair.

22. Letting Go the Painter

Directly after the siege, several senior City Police officers were reluctant to accept that the second victim had not been Peter the Painter. H Division thought differently and resumed its search for him with what the *Daily Mail* described as ''unabated vigour''. For a few days some newspapers thought him dead, others still alive, but by the week-end there was unanimity. The Painter might well have masterminded the Exchange Buildings outrage, said the *Daily Telegraph* leader of 6th January; his being still at large was ''a great public danger than if a full-grown Bengal tiger had escaped . . . from the Zoo''.

Both the two principal Press versions of how the City Police were put on to their quarry in Sidney Street referred to Fritz Svaars and Peter the Painter. On 4th and 6th January the *Daily Chronicle* published statements which it said—apparently with truth—it had obtained from a personal friend of the two men. Yet another confusion of identities is evident from these. Although the young Russian who made them reminisced about Fritz and his boon companion Peter the Painter, he went on to say that he knew the latter ''not only as Peter but also as Yoshka'' and to mention that Pyotr alias Yoshka had been lodging next to a grocer's shop in Lindley Street at the time of the Exchange Buildings murders. Josef Sokoloff is generally believed to have been living in Lindley Street then. Moreover, the personal friend maintained that he had made this man's acquaintance at the Anarchist Club and had known him intimately for over two years. Obviously this could not have been Fritz's co-lodger at 59 Grove Street, who had arrived from Paris only in the autumn of 1910.

The personal friend also produced the popular account of how Peter the Painter had become so called quite a while previously by painting the scenery for a play about Father Gapon's Revolution put on at the Jubilee Street club, whereas the Painter had been in London only about three weeks when the club closed. Since the real Peter the Painter was a painter by trade who also painted in oils as a pastime, and only his forename was generally known, the euphonious label was probably far more prosaic in origin.

The personal friend's description of Pyotr alias Yoshka resembled Rebecca Fleischmann's of Josef Sokoloff: tall and dark with a ''handsome, rather long'' face, a black moustache and ''rather curly'' black hair. Fritz and Pyotr alias Yoshka were extremely close, the personal friend declared. Pyotr alias Yoshka's character as revealed by the statements—his companionable nature, high spirits, impulsiveness and generosity when in funds—certainly sounded more likely to make them soul-mates than Fritz and the bland and cultivated Painter.

Luba Milstein was later to testify that she never saw Peter the Painter with a firearm; nor did anyone else ever speak in court of his having one. The personal friend also related this incident:

> The first time I knew that Peter carried firearms was one night a fortnight before the murders, when we were together very late by a coffee-stall in the Commercial Road. We were set upon and jostled by some English roughs, who threatened us with violence. I was for a retreat, as we were outnumbered. But Peter said ''Don't run. I will show them this!'' He pulled out of his pocket a big pistol and pointed it at our assailants, who then took to their heels.

Neither Fritz nor Pyotr alias Yoshka ''ever showed any signs of doing any honest work''. They spent much of their time at the

Jubilee Street club or playing cards in cafés, sandwich shops and gaming-houses. In this *milieu* they mixed with many professed Anarchists. "My impression is," remarked the personal friend, "that both of them used Anarchy [*sic*] as a mask for crimes of a purely personal nature." Directly he read the wanted men's descriptions, he recognized his friends.

He had had an alarming experience on Monday afternoon, 19th December, when, intending to enter the Foresters' Music Hall in Cambridge Road, he encountered Pyotr alias Yoshka also just going in. The other man obviously saw him but offered no friendly greeting. The personal friend considered giving information but, remembering Pyotr alias Yoshka's big pistol, abandoned the idea. Three days after this, shortly before the funeral procession passed along the Whitechapel Road, he had been astonished to see Fritz in Osborn Street.[1]

Josef Sokoloff's past history was typically vague and shadowy. An apprentice watchmaker in Russia, he appeared since his arrival in Britain at the turn of the century to have worked briefly for a great many employers, usually jewellers. Such young immigrants were commonly reputed to have left their native shores one jump ahead of the police, and Josef was no exception; he was wanted in the Crimea, it was rumoured, in connection with several jewel robberies. According to police information, Fritz Svaars too was a fugitive from justice, having escaped whilst in custody on suspicion of murder and robbery in Riga in 1905.

By arrangement between the Mile End Board of Guardians (who met the cost) and the City Burial Board, the pair were buried at Ilford Cemetery on 23rd January. The occasion did not pass off smoothly. The two small, plain coffins of unpolished elm each bore a thin brass plate, one inscribed "Fritz Svaars, aged twenty-seven" and the other "Josef, aged twenty-five". With several others, they were taken into the chapel in the usual way. There was a dramatic scene (the *Daily Telegraph* reported) when the chaplain arrived: it was "monstrous", he protested, that he should have to perform the Church of England burial service over these men and "an outrage upon public decency" that they

[1] See footnote on p. 63.

should have to be buried in the same ground as Bentley and Tucker. After the chapel service the offenders were removed to a communal grave in unconsecrated ground.

An attempt was made to dispose of Morountzeff's corpse even less formally. At a meeting of the St George's-in-the-East Board of Guardians on 2nd February a councillor moved that it be placed in "a rough box made from an egg box" and, if possible, sent to the council's destructor for cremation. Morountzeff's remains were not the Board's responsibility, the chairman said; the motion was out of order.

Pawn-tickets in police hands gave a fair indication of how Morountzeff and his associates kept themselves in funds. Two of the tickets covered the pledging of items of jewellery early in November by an S. Stengel of 44 Gold Street. One of the passports held by Morountzeff was a John Stenzel's. A third ticket—found in Trassjonsky's room at 10 Settles Street—referred to a gold watch pledged for £4 in the name of Charles Summerfeldt of 42 Gold Street. This transaction occurred on 16th December, the day of the murders and the day Enrico Malatesta received his £4 payment. All three articles were of German or Swiss manufacture; the Stenzel passport contained a twelve-month residence-permit granted in Hamburg early in 1909, and Morountzeff was wanted by the German police in connection with robberies there. Another gold watch and a gold seal compass had been pawned in the names of Adolf Brown of 59 Grove Street and Jane Brown of White Horse Street, Stepney.

Morountzeff was reported to be well-known in Warsaw. According to the *Daily Telegraph*'s correspondent there, the city suffered several acts of terrorism at the end of 1905 which the police believed to have been organized by a recent arrival from Russia. At the same time, the Russian police had requested them to search for a man named Murontzeff. Their investigations went to show that Murontzeff and the recent arrival were the same man.

> It was further discovered that Murontzeff had offered himself to all the advanced parties, including the 'Black Flag' group of Anarchists, as instructor for their 'fighting organizations'. His offers, however, were declined. Thereupon he collected together a number of

hooligans and thieves and organized a special party known as the *Zmowa Robotnicza* [Workers' Conspiracy], which devoted its baleful energies to robberies with violence and attacks upon banks and commercial houses. In these outrages seven persons were killed.

The Warsaw police broke up the gang, but Murontzeff eluded them. As his behaviour comprised the revolutionary movement, the *Telegraph* report concluded, endeavours were made to 'remove' him; he killed two Social Democrats in one of these. One way and another, he had made the Polish capital too hot to hold him. He was thought to have fled the country in 1907.

If Morountzeff had led the Exchange Buildings criminals, and Fritz and Josef had been his principal henchmen, what part had the elusive Peter the Painter played? The question provoked endless speculation. Music-hall references to him brought instant laughter and applause; newspapers concocted laborious puns: the police would not let go the Painter if they could help it, the *Star* joked. Many of his acquaintances were emphatic that he was not the type to be concerned in shootings, it remarked.

As January drew to a close, the belief that the Painter had escaped gained ground. The police were understandably loth to accept that their bird had flown, and new material about him— the contents of two dossiers, one in the records of the Marseilles criminal detective department and the other of the Paris police's Anarchist Brigade—revived public interest in finding him for a while. On 30th January Old Jewry issued a new £500-reward handbill almost entirely devoted to him. It reproduced two three-quarter-length photographs of him supplied by Marseilles and, for the first time, gave his full name as Peter Piatkow (Piaktow), alias Schtern.

His description was virtually unchanged. The categorical statement that he was Russian surprised many people who took him for a German or a Frenchman. "He is a man of striking and even intelligent appearance," the *Daily Telegraph* remarked, noting also that, while tall, he lacked Morountzeff's muscular build. The photographs showed him wearing a moustache and an imperial, but he was thought not to have had a beard on the night of 16th December.

He was known to have been imprisoned in his own country for

offences committed during the 1905 uprising. Both the French police files described him as an associate of terrorists, but neither attributed any terrorist activity to him personally. Marseilles named him as Peter Piatkoff (Piaktoff), born in Pskoff—a town about 175 miles north-east of Riga—on 20th June 1883. He had disembarked at the French port from Oran in April 1908 and, the police having been informed that his companions were terrorists, was soon under surveillance.

Piaktoff, who usually went by the German or Jewish name of Schtern, was the son of a farmer and the nephew of an army colonel. He first studied at the Marseilles school of medicine but later became a house-painter. He had a succession of lodgings in the city, which he eventually left for Evian-les-Bains (on Lake Geneva) in January 1910. "All the time he lived at Marseilles," a Press report from there observed, "Peter the Painter never attracted any notice. He worked steadily and never had any trouble with the police." A subsequent Marseilles report added that in June 1909 Piaktoff had witnessed a fatal accident. The clarity and style of his lengthy formal statement, made in the purest French, had astonished the examining magistrate.

According to the Paris dossier, he spoke not only Russian and French but German, Yiddish and English. The police had come across Peter Piaktoff in 1908, it said, when searching the home of one of a group of Anarchists following an incident at Maisons-Alfort railway station.[2] Whilst Marseilles reported that he had "resided some time" in Evian, Paris was specific that he had lodged in the capital's 14th Arrondissement from December 1909 to October 1910, when he left for London. Neither in Paris nor in Marseilles was any evidence found of his having returned after the Exchange Buildings murders.

As the weeks went by, police forces in various parts of the world claimed to have found the Painter. His total evaporation, with his unknown role likely to remain so, caused much frustration. It seems that ex-Detective Sergeant Leeson's unconscious mind developed a craving for further contact with him and his friends. Writing in his reminiscences nearly twenty-five years

---

[2] Maisons-Alfort lies in the Marne Valley, about 10 miles from Paris.

later about his Australian visit, Leeson described at length how he had managed to evade two men who tried to meet him when his ship put in at Albany and again in Melbourne. In reality they were probably journalists; Leeson was convinced that they represented "the arm of Anarchism and Petrograd, of Bolshevism and Moscow".[3] His extremely melodramatic and unreliable version of the Exchange Buildings case clearly reveals his abnormal state of mind.

Another of Leeson's stories has circulated for many years. Having decided that while in Melbourne he must visit the Blue Mountains, who should he catch sight of in the Central Station booking-hall but Peter the Painter. Leeson had a compartment to himself; the same man got in at a wayside halt soon after the train left Melbourne and accompanied him for the rest of his journey. Leeson thought furiously about the suspicions that might be in Peter's mind and the loaded pistol that was almost certainly in his pocket; the two men exchanged a little small-talk, and nothing remotely untoward took place. The idea of a subsequent meeting of this kind is so attractive that, if such a story did not already exist, there was almost a necessity to invent one. No doubt this is precisely what the ex-sergeant unwittingly did.

With the realization that the Painter had slipped through their fingers, the police faced another unpalatable fact: even if he were found, they possessed no evidence that he had fired any shots in Exchange Buildings on 16th December or had even been there at the time. The chances of obtaining his extradition would therefore be negligible, and no commonsense alternative existed so far as he was concerned but to let matters rest.

And so, as the first weeks of 1911 became months, Peter the Painter passed out of currency into memory. Many years later, having consulted the City Police about what became of him, J. P. Eddy reported that "There is in fact correspondence from official Russian sources which shows that he returned to Russia after 1910. In fact, in December 1912 he was wanted by the Russian police for evading military service, and he was then said to have

---

[3] Ex-Detective Sergeant B. Leeson, *Lost London* (Stanley Paul, 1934), p. 219. St Petersburg was later to be renamed first Petrograd and then Leningrad.

absconded to Germany, but his exact whereabouts were said to be unknown."[4]

The search for Joe Levi (otherwise Max Smoller) was also intensified at the end of January, but without avail. Nott-Bower later wrote that both men escaped to France.

Two of the fourteen distinguishable characters thought to have been implicated in the Exchange Buildings crimes were now presumed to be abroad. In view of the evidence difficulty, neither was pursued. In addition, three had died, and the number of others secured and charged had risen early in February from five to eight. This left one man with whom the police were convinced there was a score to settle: Enrico Malatesta. Emphasizing in his memoirs the practical assistance Morountzeff had had from the fiery Italian aristocrat, Nott-Bower admitted defeat but hinted at Nemesis merely postponed: "But there was insufficient evidence to prove guilty knowledge of the premeditated burglary. He was, however, convicted of another offence at the Central Criminal Court in 1912 and recommended for deportation."[5] This is true—as far as it goes. On 20th May 1912 Malatesta, who had suggested in a circular to Italians living in London that a fellow expatriate was an Italian police spy, was found guilty of criminal libel. His defence and character entirely failed to impress the Common Serjeant, who sentenced him to three months' imprisonment, ordered him to pay the prosecution costs and recommended his expulsion as an undesirable alien. He was also refused bail pending his appeal.

This severity shocked the defendant's Radical and Labour sympathizers, Ramsay MacDonald and Keir Hardie amongst them. No time was lost mounting a crusade. Two days after his conviction, Malatesta figured in a Commons debate on political offences; the Home Secretary (then Reginald McKenna) was plied with questions, and demonstrations were held in Trafalgar Square. On 17th June, after the Italian's appeal had gone against him, McKenna told the House he had decided not to comply with the court's recommendation. "I did not think that an

[4] *Op. cit.*, p. 30.

[5] *Op. cit.*, p. 232.

expulsion order was required in the public interest," he explained later.

Efforts to have the prison sentence quashed as well proved unavailing. Malatesta returned to his native land before and after the war, reviving the animosity of the Italian police with typically inflammatory speeches.

PART IV
Legal Process

23. Six Bullets from a Dreyse

The twin East London and City inquests into the Exchange Buildings murders continued alongside the Guildhall hearings until 9th and 10th February respectively. Although the police evidence, understandably enough, was often confused and even contradictory, a reasonably coherent account of events and their probable sequence gradually crystallized. The gist of Inspector Bryant's version of them follows:

> I was standing with Sergeant Tucker in the carriageway, 5 or 6 yards from no. 11 on the Cutler Street side, when I saw Sergeant Bentley knock at the door. I did not see it opened but knew it had been from what he said. Bentley looked round at us and said "A foreigner." I approached him, and as I did so, he stepped inside the house. I then noticed the lower part of a man standing on the stairs; I could also see into the parlour.
>
> I heard Bentley ask the man on the stairs, "Is anyone working at the back?" He replied, "No." Bentley said, "Is anyone making a noise out there?" The man again said, "No." Bentley then asked, "Can we have a look out at the back?" The man answered, "Yes." Bentley said, "Will you show us the way?" The man pointed to the parlour doorway and said, "In there."
>
> At this, Bentley moved to the right into the parlour doorway, and I stepped from the pavement into the passage. I then saw a man come in from the back of the room and pass between Bentley and the table. He had a pistol in his hand and at once began to fire towards Bentley's right shoulder. I heard three or four shots fired very rapidly; I was hit and fell out on to the pavement.

Constable Martin, the plain-clothes patrolman, had already identified Morountzeff as the man who opened the door to Bentley; Bryant now identified him as the other man who had rushed into the parlour from the back. Bryant added that this other man's pistol had struck him as long and black, with only

one barrel—a recognizable description of a Mauser; later, however, he produced a Dreyse automatic which he said resembled
it. He had been unable to see the face of the man on the stairs, nor
could he say whether he too had fired.

Constable Strongman, the other plain-clothes patrolman
present, continued Bryant's story:

> I was standing beside Sergeant Tucker and heard several shots fired.
> We took a step towards the door of no. 11, and Sergeant Bentley fell
> through it. I saw a hand, holding a pistol and firing rapidly, protrude
> from the door. The firing was at Constable Woodhams, who was on
> the other side of Exchange Buildings, and I saw him fall towards the
> carriageway. Then a man came out of the doorway, still holding the
> pistol and pointing it at Tucker and myself. He was firing rapidly all
> the time; we retreated a few yards as it was impossible to get hold of
> him.
>
> Tucker staggered. Seeing he was hit, I put my arm round him and
> led him away towards Cutler Street. As I did so, I looked back over
> my left shoulder; the man fired two more shots in our direction. I
> could also see more flashes coming from the doorway, where
> someone else was firing. The man who had been firing at us turned
> and went back towards no. 11.

Strongman was positive this man was Morountzeff. His first
description of the man's weapon also fitted a Mauser; he saw its
barrel as the man came near the street-lamp, he said, and it
looked long and thin. Subsequently shown a Belgian Browning
automatic, however, he then said it had been similar to this. The
two squat little automatics were of course vastly different in
appearance from the great Mausers. "I hope I may never have to
observe the kind of pistol with which a person is firing at me,"
senior Treasury counsel was to remark later.

Martin's evidence differed little from that of Bryant and
Strongman. After Bentley had talked with him, the man who had
opened the front door then closed it to about an inch and disappeared behind it, apparently going upstairs. He had not gone
into the parlour. Bentley had then pushed the front door open
and entered, crossing to the right and standing with one foot in
the passage and the other in the parlour, which was very well lit.
About a minute later the back door flew open, and a man rushed
in from the yard. Directly he began firing, a shot came from the

stairs, which were in darkness. Martin had seen only the extended forearm, hand and pistol of this man who rushed in; he did not think this man's hand was the same as the one he and Strongman had both seen a few seconds later projecting through the front doorway. The pistol in this latter hand had looked "bright", he added. Seeing it swinging round in his direction, he turned swiftly and ducked, losing his balance and falling into the carriageway.

Just as he fell, Martin said, he heard something strike the house opposite. Ada Parker, of 2 Exchange Buildings, later testified that a bullet had crossed their parlour, cutting a leg of her mother's chair and making a hole in her skirt. Two more bullets entered no. 3, which was unoccupied.

Examination of the two bullet-holes in Sergeant Bentley's helmet showed the entrance-hole at the front to be higher than the rear exit one, suggesting that the bullet must have been fired from the stairs above him. From the almost horizontal, right-to-left path which the two bullets that hit him had taken after entering his body, it was concluded that these had been fired from the right-hand side of the parlour.

The Crown's last important witness at Guildhall was Ernest Goodwin, MA(Cantab), assistant to the chief superintendent of Eley Brothers, the well-known cartridge-makers, and the firearms-expert on the case. It was not possible at that time to identify the individual weapon from which a bullet had been fired, only its particular type. Goodwin's conclusions may be summarized as follows:

> Three different types of firearm were used in the Exchange Buildings affray: the Dreyse and the Belgian Browning 7·65mm pistols, which fire a standard ammunition, and the Mauser ·30 pistol, which fires a special cartridge.[1]
>
> The Dreyse found in the bedding under Morountzeff's pillow had been recently fired. This make of pistol has a distinctive barrel-rifling which features four grooves. The two bullets extracted from Tucker's body, the two from Bentley's body and the two undamaged ones from Choat's trunk all bore the marks of these grooves; all six

---

[1] Bodkin demonstrated in his opening statement at Guildhall that at least twenty-two shots must have been fired.

bullets must therefore have been fired by this pistol or one of similar pattern and manufacture.

The only other undamaged bullet retained by Choat's body was a ·30 taken from his leg. Two of the three bullets fired into 2 and 3 Exchange Buildings and the two fired into the parlour ceiling at no. 11 were also of this calibre. These bullets bore marks corresponding with the rifling of the two Mausers found at 100 Sidney Street.[2]

The bullet recovered from Morountzeff's body was a 7·65mm one bearing five groove marks. Five such grooves characterize the rifling of the Belgian Browning.

There was no lack of other evidence—such as Constable Piper's certainty that it was he that had opened the door of no. 11 so suspiciously twenty-five minutes before the shooting—incriminating Morountzeff. The musician Tocmacoff identified one of the Sidney Street Mausers as having been in Fritz Svaars's possession; Fritz had shown it to him (no doubt with characteristic panache) one day at 59 Grove Street. Josef Sokoloff, the third man, remained an enigma.

The lack of evidence against Luba Milstein led to her discharge on 22nd February. Karl Hoffmann, the sailor and paperhanger, having been detained on 8th February and charged with conspiring to rob, was freed four weeks later for the same reason. Before the Guildhall proceedings finally ended, both gave evidence for the defence.

Neatly dressed in a blue costume and wearing a long fur, Luba underwent a rigorous cross-examination by Bodkin. Parts of her story have already been told; the gist of the remainder follows:

I first heard about the policemen being murdered at 5 p.m. on 17th December from an acquaintance at 36 Havering Street. The statement I made after being detained next day was not entirely true; I was afraid of implicating myself in some way, also of betraying Fritz, Josef, Peter and Max.

I first became acquainted with Fritz five or six months before I was detained. I also knew Hoffmann at this time; he went by the name of Chochol. Max was one of Fritz's visitors at New Castle Place. His

---

[2] Every Mauser bore a maker's serial number; those of the Sidney Street pair were 66,443 and 66,531. Fritz Svaars was said to have acquired his in Antwerp, but how Josef Sokoloff came by the other, if known, was not disclosed. It will be noticed that the serial numbers were less than a hundred apart out of 66,500.

callers at 59 Grove Street included Hoffmann, who was a close friend of his, Josef, Morountzeff, Duboff, Peters and Rosen. Peters came very seldom. Josef was tall and dark, with black hair; he did not limp but always carried one shoulder higher than the other. Sometimes, when Morountzeff or Josef came, I would not be allowed into the front room.

At midnight on 16th December I was lying on the bed in the back room reading a book. Rosie Trassjonsky was with me and Peter was in the front room. I heard two or three people run up the stairs; they went into the front room, and, wondering what was the matter, I knocked at the door. Fritz called out to me not to come in. Max appeared and asked "Where is Fritz?" I replied "In the front room," and he went in. Fritz came out in a very excited state and asked me for a sovereign he had given me a week before. I handed it to him, and he told me to "go away somewhere." I heard him say to Rosie, "Morountzeff is wounded. Will you be so kind as to put some cold water to his side?" I saw Josef in the passage.

The men were in the house only two or three minutes. I went into the front room after they had gone and saw Morountzeff lying on the bed. A quarter of an hour after they left, not knowing where else to go, I went to Hoffmann's room at 36 Lindley Street, where I saw Fritz, Peter and Josef. Josef was holding a long pistol. Fritz told me that he had carried Morountzeff in his arms like a baby, and that when they came near the Commercial Road, he (Fritz) had intended leaving him there; however, Morountzeff began screaming, and they were compelled to carry him further. Nothing was said about Josef's pistol, and I did not ask about it; they would not allow me to stay a minute.

Hoffmann's account of events on the night of 16th December bore out Luba's:

I went to bed at twelve o'clock and was woken up by Josef, who had a Mauser pistol. He said that Max had shot Poolka. There had been a fight somewhere. Two or three minutes later, Fritz came in by himself. He had two pistols, another Mauser and a Browning. A few minutes after that Peter the Painter arrived, also alone, and a little after him Luba Milstein.

Fritz took out the Browning and said "I must see if it is fully loaded."[3] He said that Max had helped him carry Morountzeff to

---

[3] This remark has been attributed to bloodthirstiness—which could be mistaken. Morountzeff had been shot in the back in a confused *mêlée*, and a great deal must

Grove Street, given him the Browning and left. He did not know where Max had gone. He had meant to leave Morountzeff at the corner of the Commercial Road, but Morountzeff began to cry out.

They told me they had come to stay all night. I said that, if they did, I would go. I got up to dress, and they all went. I have not seen any of these men since.

The East London jury took fifteen minutes to decide that Tucker had been murdered by Morountzeff, and Choat and Morountzeff by some person or persons unknown. The conclusions of the City jury, reached the following day, were that Bentley had been killed by Morountzeff while he and others unnamed were engaged in an attempt at shopbreaking and that those others were thus equally guilty of his murder.

24. The Barber, the Paperhanger and the Cigarette-Maker

One purpose of the continuing police enquiries was of course to secure further evidence against the accused. The prosecution case, which Bodkin—prevented by defence counsels' vigorous protests from putting off his opening any longer—spent 1½ hours outlining at Guildhall on 23rd January, sorely needed some. The evidence would show, he claimed, that the attempted robbery was "a long-concerted and very carefully planned scheme" and that amongst the nine or ten persons concerned in it, "each of them taking different but yet important parts", were the five prisoners. His summary scarcely mentioned them, however; its principal characters were not before the court and, apart from Isaac Levy's firm identification of Peters and Duboff, the association between the absentees and the dejected men and

have been said on the journey to Grove Street with him about who was to blame. No doubt Max was extremely frightened; he may well have denied shooting him or even firing at all. Had the Browning still been fully loaded, obviously he could not have done and—if the reconstruction in the Author's Notes is correct—the culprit would have had to be Fritz himself.

women in the dock remained unrevealed as anything more than social.

"What would you expect to happen where there are several persons, each to play different parts in such a scheme, but a meeting to arrange the last details?" Bodkin asked the court. Although Morountzeff had probably discussed final arrangements with his confederates at the Grove Street gathering on 16th December, Bodkin's close examination of his first witness, the musician Tocmacoff, provided no evidence whatever implicating the accused in their conspiracy. Jacob Peters had not even been there.

He had never seen Peter the Painter with a pistol, Tocmacoff remarked. Bodkin derided the idea of Fritz, an alien without employment himself, helping Fedoroff find work, but Tocmacoff could not agree. He knew Fedoroff was looking for work everywhere, and Fritz knew so many people. The musician and Duboff together had talked over their job-prospects with Fritz. Small as Fritz's influence might have been in reality, all this rang true. It was also odd that Fedoroff and Duboff should have been so anxious to find work if just about to share in the proceeds of a lucrative robbery.

Bodkin had little help from most of his witnesses, who, when not actually unforthcoming, tended to be vague and casual. Questioned at length about events at 59 Grove Street, Lizzie Katz was noticeably unhelpful, and Mark contradicted her evidence and his own a number of times. Several minor points of interest emerged, however: Fritz was the only one of their three lodgers whose name they knew; Lizzie had received their 7s.6d rent on Saturday evenings from Fritz or his 'wife', never the other man; sometimes Fritz would speak of their being out late at a concert, and the front door would be left unbolted. Mark had never asked the trio anything about themselves: "It was nothing to do with me. They paid their rent, or else they would have had to get out." Lizzie had never even spoken to Trassjonsky. She saw nothing sinister about the two young men Dr Scanlan had met on his second visit; her husband worked with several who came to see him now and then.

From the evidence of the landlord's manager, it was clear that 9 and 11 Exchange Buildings had been taken, and their rent subsequently paid, by Joe Levi, Morountzeff and a third man— almost certainly Fritz Svaars from his description—acting in conjunction. No. 10 had stood empty since early in December, but two or three days before the affray the landlords moved some goods into it for temporary storage. Their storekeeper later told the court that he was at the house between 7 and 7.30 on the evening of the murders, taking them out again. Having finished, he shut the front door with a bang, whereupon no. 11's front door opened and a woman looked out. Two hours later, Max Weil's maidservant was listening to the noises that brought Piper to the scene.

Isaac Levy was recalled. He described the woman he had seen with the three men immediately after the murders as 5 feet 4 or 5 inches tall, nice-looking, wearing a toque and carrying a fashionable muff. F. J. Maw, a quick-witted and exceptionally tenacious young solicitor now defending all three male accused, crossexamined severely; Levy sparred with him. He had not been frightened by the encounter, he insisted, but it upset him: "I haven't had it off my mind since." Levy could not give an accurate description of how Peters and Duboff had been dressed, nor could he say which had been on Morountzeff's right and which on his left. He agreed that their line-up had contained only about five foreigners. If seven other witnesses testified to the two men having been elsewhere at the time, Maw asked him, would he still insist that his identification of them was not a mistake? Levy refused to be shaken.

Called upon by Maw to produce Levy's signed statement to the police, Bodkin declined to do so. Maw tried again to bring out this statement at a later sitting and was again rebuffed; it was no part of his duty to supply the defence with such material, Bodkin asserted.

Mr Maw (to Sir W. Treloar): "I ask you, sir, to say it would be only fair that it should be produced."

Sir W. Treloar: "I use my own words, sir, and not yours. I have said I can make no order."

Shortly before the two inquests ended, the police apprehended three more suspects. John Rosen, alias Zelin, was taken from the hairdresser's shop at 112 Well Street, Hackney, where he lived and worked, on 2nd February; a twenty-three-year-old Russian girl called Lena (or Nina) Vassileva was arrested while walking in Sidney Street on 7th February, and Karl Hoffmann was picked up early the following morning. None of the three had a firearm or attempted any resistance.

Rosen, who was twenty-six and had lived in London for two years, had been married only forty-eight hours when Detective Inspector Newell detained him. He professed ignorance at first but changed his mind and volunteered a statement on 5th February. He was not charged until 8th February, and then only with conspiracy to rob. Flaxen-haired, pale and vivacious, Vassileva was described as a native of Ekaterinoslav in South Russia and a cigarette-maker, of 11 Buross Street. (Buross Street is a turning south out of the Commercial Road.) The identification-parades in which she and Hoffmann took part were scrupulously correct; a Russian consular official attended and expressed his satisfaction. Isaac Levy identified her as the woman he had met with Morountzeff and his two accomplices just after the shooting. The charges against her, preferred only forty-eight hours after Newell had arrested her also, were both of conspiring to rob and of being concerned in the murders. She knew nothing of Exchange Buildings or these three men, Vassileva declared with spirit.

Rosen admitted knowing everyone concerned in the case. Apart from Jacob Peters, whom he had not seen since the previous summer, he had met them casually from time to time at various lodging-houses. Hoffmann, whom he knew as Masais, was his particular crony amongst them. He admitted visiting 59 Grove Street on 16th December; he had met Hoffmann in the Commercial Road soon after 2 p.m., he said, and had gone there with him at his suggestion. Hoffmann was then living at 36 Lindley Street, and Rosen described a visit there on Sunday, 18th December, when Hoffmann had told him guardedly about his four midnight visitors of two nights before and what had passed between them.

Rosen had also called on Vassileva at 11 Buross Street two or three days after the murders. The gist of his account of this meeting follows:

I had no object in going to see her. She said, "Have you brought trouble with you?" and I replied, "I don't know." She was pouring something on her hair out of a bottle and then brushing it. It was partly brown and partly black. I gathered that she had dyed it, but the dye was not good, and she was washing it out again. I was there only ten or fifteen minutes; she seemed reluctant to talk to me and told me not to come again as I might bring some trouble.

Lena said she was the woman who had been living at Exchange Buildings and that she left when the two men went in. I understood this to mean when they went in to commit the robbery.

He had never been in Exchange Buildings, Rosen's statement concluded, nor had he known that anyone he mentioned intended committing any crime. Newell testified to having taken possession of a blue serge three-quarter-length coat which he found in Vassileva's room after her arrest. When Isaac Levy confirmed his identification of her, Vassileva became very excited. "He is a lying witness!" she exclaimed angrily.

Numerous people testified to seeing Morountzeff, Peter the Painter and various accused apart from Milstein and Hoffmann in or near Exchange Buildings before the murders. No photographs being available of Fritz Svaars and Josef Sokoloff in either life or death, similar identification of them was impossible. Three of the most prominent of these witnesses, fourteen-year-old Solomon Abrahams and two young clerks named Richardson and Crook, were close friends who had worked for the same employer. Well over half the alleged sightings had occurred in Houndsditch, Aldgate and suchlike places of popular resort; everyone thus identified either lived nearby or had friends who did, and a sinister construction could not reasonably be placed on them.

There was one notable exception, however. Richardson described an incident which he said took place late in the evening of 30th November while his employer at 16 Houndsditch was at a police boxing-competition. He was standing at the shop door when Morountzeff, who was with Vassileva and another man (probably Josef Sokoloff) whom Richardson could not identify, came by and engaged him in casual conversation. The talk came round to the jeweller next door to no. 16 and to Harris's. Morountzeff remarked that he understood Harris's to be a very good shop for diamonds and wondered whether Mr Harris lived on the premises. Richardson replied shortly that he could not say; Morountzeff should ask Mr Harris.

Crook confirmed this story. He did not recognize any of the accused except Vassileva, but Richardson claimed to have seen all of them except Milstein and Hoffmann in the Exchange Buildings neighbourhood on different dates. Maw attacked Richardson's testimony and credibility with some success. Would he persist in his claim to have seen Duboff in Cutler Street and Aldgate in the face of witnesses who would say Duboff was working miles away at the time? Certainly, Richardson replied.

He had lived in Exchange Buildings all his life, Solomon Abrahams told the court. He claimed to have noticed Morountzeff, Peter the Painter, Vassileva, Trassjonsky, Duboff and Rosen in the cul-de-sac on various occasions. Cross-examination made him aggressive, and defence counsel succeeded in tripping him up several times over matters of detail. Trassjonsky had said she did not even know where Exchange Buildings was, her counsel pointed out to the boy, and he had had a good look at her at 59 Grove Street before formally identifying her at the police station. Was he really sure he had seen her? Solomon was positive.

The Crown had not found such certain identification of members of the group, other than Morountzeff and Vassileva, easy to come by. Constable Piper, for example, could only say that Duboff "resembled" the pale-faced, fair-haired man he had noticed standing in Cutler Street looking down Exchange Buildings as he left no. 11 after talking to Morountzeff. The asbestos sheets and 4-foot deal box found at 9 Exchange Buildings had been traced back, but the supplier of the asbestos could only pick out Peters as "very much resembling" his customer, and the box-maker identified nobody. The contractor's men who had seen four "foreigners" cross Petticoat Lane and pass through Wentworth Street immediately after the shooting were unable to identify Morountzeff, Peters or Duboff as having been among them. The pawnbroker's assistant who had handled the Charles Summerfeldt transaction of 16 December could not recognize any of the accused.

No. 1 Exchange Buildings was used for selling second-hand

goods, and Joseph Dacosta, general factotum there, said that Vassileva had once asked him to clean the windows of no. 11. He had seen her taking down no. 11's shutters in the morning and putting them up in the evening every day for about a fortnight. One shutter, the middle one, was always left up. Her hair was much darker then than when he first identified her. "That ain't the hair what she had," he commented in court, nodding in Vassileva's direction. The manager of the 'Cutlers' Arms' said he had seen Vassileva sweeping out no. 11's parlour; her hair was then dark brown.

The fragility of much of the prosecution's sighting-evidence was clearly demonstrated when Bessie Jacobs, the seventeen-year-old girl at no. 5, came under examination. An attempt by Bessie, who also spoke of having seen Vassileva taking down the shutters each morning, to identify one of the men facing her in court ended ignominiously. She admitted attending a number of identification-parades before picking out Peters as a man she had seen in Exchange Buildings several times wearing a slouch hat. The male prisoners having been told to put on their hats, she said she had made a mistake: it was not Peters but Fedoroff she recognized—though only when he had a hat on. Later on, in re-examination, she told Bodkin she had first seen this man four or five months previously.

When Bessie's evidence about Vassileva was translated, Trassjonsky made one of her occasional enigmatic interjections. "I am the woman, not her," she exclaimed.

25. A Perfectly Respectable Young Woman

In Hoffmann's possession when he was detained were the return half of a tourist ticket between London and Antwerp, a Russian passport in the name of Trokhimchik and a dagger. An extremely guarded statement he had made was more remarkable for its lies and omissions than for fresh information. Born in Libau in 1887, he had first visited London about five years previously; when not at sea, he stayed sometimes there and sometimes in France, Holland or elsewhere. After his arrival in London seven months earlier, he had lived at 36 Lindley Street and worked as a paper-hanger with a man called Gordon of 11 Buross Street.

Hoffmann admitted having "seen" most of the people in the case and having visited Fritz at 59 Grove Street several times. "The first time I went there, I wanted to go into the front room, but I was not allowed to go in there—I don't know the reason—so I never tried to go after that." He had never been visited by Rosen. On the night of 16th December he went to the moving pictures, returned home at about nine o'clock and played chess with his landlord. He did not go out again and went to bed about midnight. He had no visitors during the night. Two days after the Sidney Street affair, he left Lindley Street and went to Antwerp.[1]

The rest of the prosecution evidence was dominated by that of Isaac Gordon and his wife and daughter. An elderly Jewish paperhanger who had settled in London fourteen years before, Isaac could not read and had no English. Vassileva had lived at 11 Buross Street with him, Annie and twelve-year-old Polly since April 1910. The substance of his story follows:

[1] Hoffmann claimed to have left of his own volition, but his landlord, Woolf Brown, later told the court that he gave his lodger notice. No doubt Brown was alive to the possibility of his house suffering a fate similar to 100 Sidney Street's.

I have known Hoffmann for three years, and it was he who recommended Lena as a lodger. She was a perfectly respectable young woman, quiet, well-behaved and friendly. She occupied the back ground-floor room, going out to work and sometimes bringing work home. She said she earned 30 shillings a week. Hoffmann, Duboff (who has also worked for me) and Rosen all called on her. Another visitor was Morountzeff, whose name I did not know. I last saw Hoffmann and Rosen two or three weeks after the shooting.

Six or seven weeks before Christmas, Lena said that she was going to look after a woman friend called Mascha who was sick. She stayed away three weeks, calling occasionally for clean clothes. She then announced that she would be away another two or three weeks because her employer was ill and she had to manage his business. Her hair at this time was its normal flaxen colour. This was the last we saw of her until the evening of Saturday, 17th December.

The gas-meter was in Lena's room, and not knowing she had returned, I went in to put a penny into it. She was sitting on the floor surrounded by papers, some of which she was tearing up and throwing on the fire. I did not recognize her at first; her hair was black. Her mistress where she had been had dyed her hair, she said, and she had done the same. I did not believe this. I called my wife, who was also very taken aback. "Don't burn any papers," I told Lena, "because it makes a bad smell. Give me the papers, and I will keep them for you." Lena told me she had heard about the shooting and was afraid to keep them as she believed the police would call at every house. Subsequently she handed them over to me.

Next morning I found her looking at a newspaper and weeping. She said that a particular friend of hers had been accidentally shot by a companion. "They had better have shot me than him," she added. "I know what a man he has been." I understood him to have been her lover. She told me that she was not at the shooting, having left the place at five o'clock.

Amongst Vassileva's papers were several books, a false passport and about a dozen photographs. Suspicious and anxious, Isaac called on his brother-in-law in Sidney Square with them that same day, Sunday, 18th December. On his brother-in-law's advice he then took them to Arbour Square police-station.

On Monday Lena tried unsuccessfully to persuade another friend to let her stay at his house for a time. On Tuesday she declared that "London was not made for her"; she would go to Paris. She again went out and came back, explaining this time that she could not leave because the police were watching her. Whatever happened, she said, she would stay where she was.

Lena kept to the house for about three weeks after this, only going out to a nearby shop for the spirit with which she kept washing and rewashing her hair. "When I get it clean," she remarked, "I shall not be afraid of anyone. If I go to the place where the shooting affair occurred, I am lost for ever. They would recognize me. If I get prison here, it would not be so bad. If I am sent back to Russia, I'll get hung."

On the Wednesday I smelled paraffin and went into her room. She was burning a hat and a blue skirt, which were saturated with it. The curtains had also been burnt. Lena went away again a week before her arrest, saying she was going to stay with some friends.

Annie Gordon corroborated much of her husband's evidence and added a little of her own:

Lena was wretched after her return and kept remarking how grieved she was at Morountzeff's death. She spoke about the dead and injured policemen too but expressed no sympathy for them. After the idea of going to Paris had fallen through, she spent a great deal of time 'throwing cards'—telling her fortune. [Vassileva shook with laughter when this was interpreted to her.]

I saw a muff and furs in Lena's room when she came home. I had never seen her with furs before. She said they were a present from Mascha and had cost £3. When I pressed her for her rent during the following week, she asked me if I would take them in pledge until she found work.

On the evening of 17th December, young Polly told the court, Vassileva sent her out for a newspaper and asked her to read aloud the account of the Exchange Buildings affair. It described a woman the police were looking for. Vassileva became depressed and measured herself, commenting that she was exactly the height mentioned.

He had received Vassileva's papers from Isaac on 18th December and interviewed her at 11 Buross Street the same day, Detective Inspector Wensley said.[2] She was only partly dressed,

---

[2] In the witness-box but not in his memoirs, which alleged that he (not Newell) arrested Vassileva, continued with an account of the interview which omitted the date of it and ended with the statement that she was handed over to the City Police. The impression was thus conveyed that the interview took place not on

and her long hair, which was still down, was obviously dyed. She admitted having visited the Jubilee Street club sometimes. Some of the men concerned in the shooting were believed to have been members, the inspector told her; did she know them? "Perhaps I do, perhaps I don't," Vassileva replied pertly. Wensley manoeuvred her into inviting him to search the room; amongst her clothes were a dark blue three-quarter-length jacket and skirt answering the official description. When he showed her a group photograph which included Morountzeff, she said she did not know anyone in it.

Vassileva's prospects deteriorated even further when Detective Chief Inspector Collins, the fingerprint chief at Scotland Yard, gave his evidence. Collins had found on the two bottles taken from 11 Exchange Buildings two impressions of a right forefinger and one of a right thumb. Since her arrest, he had taken Vassileva's fingerprints; the ones on the bottles were unquestionably hers.

Fritz Svaars's landlady at 35 New Castle Place, Mrs Esther Goodman, and another resident, Abraham Smolensky, gave evidence about Svaars's two-month stay there. Both said they had known him as Trokhimchik—the name in the passport found in Hoffmann's possession. Their story of the innumerable visits paid to Fritz and Luba by other members of the group much resembled Woolf Brown's account of callers on Hoffmann (whom he too knew as Masais) at 36 Lindley Street. It was noteworthy that Jacob Peters had not been a visitor at either address. Since 16th December Brown had seen only his lodger and Rosen. Smolensky referred to a strong facial resemblance between Fritz and Rosen; Fritz had once pointed Rosen out jokingly as his brother. This likeness, particularly in profile, was later confirmed by Hoffmann.

Nobody had spoken of seeing Hoffmann in the vicinity of Exchange Buildings, and only two people—Solomon Abrahams and his friend Richardson—of seeing Trassjonsky. On learning

18th December but when she was finally arrested. Wensley was not the kind of man to muddle such basic facts, even twenty years afterwards; presumably the reason for this deception was a reluctance to reveal that Vassileva had been used as a decoy. (*Op. cit.*, pp. 165, 166.)

that the prosecution's case was now complete, Sir William Treloar discharged both. He considered the evidence against them insufficient, he said. Trassjonsky broke down and sobbed hysterically when told she was free.

Regarding the main charge against Peters and Duboff, the prosecution decided to stand firm on Isaac Levy's identification of them. They were accessories in such a way as to be liable to be tried for the murders, Bodkin argued, and the indictment should contain the original charge of being concerned in them. He defined the relevant principle: "Where the persons go out for an unlawful purpose in combination, and in the course of that combination it is determined to offer violent resistance to any who may hinder them in effecting that purpose, and in the course of offering such resistance a murder is committed by one of the combination, it is a murder in regard to all." Treloar assented, and the clerk read out the charges on which the prosecution sought committal: against Peters and Duboff, of murdering Sergeant Tucker; against Peters, Duboff and Vassileva, two counts of accessory after the fact; and against all five prisoners, of conspiring to rob Harris's shop.

Maw was highly critical of the evidence against Fedoroff. Counsel had spoken of each prisoner's important part in the conspiracy; what, then, was this man's? Treloar conceded the point and discharged him.

Maw then presented witnesses for Jacob Peters's defence. Louis Jonas, manager of the wholesale clothiers in Spitalfields for whom (as Jacob Colnin) Peters had worked since July 1910, testified to his being a good workman. He was steady and respectable and had been absent only two afternoons during this time. His hours were 8 a.m. to 7.30 p.m. (2 p.m. on Saturdays), and for a full week's work he was paid £1.4s. He had worked the whole day of the murders, leaving at about eight o'clock, and returned as usual next morning. His manner then was quite normal. For several weeks prior to 16th December he had earned full wages. His last payment was £1 for five days' work from Saturday, 17th December, to Thursday, 22nd December, the day he was detained; this was sent to him at Brixton Prison in the name of J. Peters-Colnin.

With Peters's landlord, Philip Abrahams, at 48 Turner Street lived his wife Bluma, their six (very shortly to be seven) children, Peters and three other lodgers. The substance of his evidence follows:

> Peters came to live at my house about four weeks before the murders. I went out between 8.30 and 9 p.m. on 16th December, and as I did so, he came in. When I returned an hour later, he opened the door to me. My wife and I watched him set a mouse-trap. There was nothing unusual about him. I did not see him after ten o'clock. I bolted the front door at 11.30 and went to bed.
>
> We sleep late on the Sabbath. While still in bed next morning, I heard someone leave the house; the street door was banged rather loudly. This happened at Peters's usual time for going to work, and he would have unbolted the door. Nobody else was up.
>
> I do not recognize Morountzeff as ever having called on Peters, and I knew nothing of Fritz Svaars until after the murders. Had I ever seen a firearm in Peters's possession, I would have given information about it.

Peters's room was a ground-floor one with its window opening on to the street; he had no watertight alibi.

First of four witnesses for Duboff was Joseph Backs, jobforeman of the painters and decorators he had worked for until 12th December. Backs's time-sheets would show, Maw said, that Duboff was working elsewhere on various dates when Crown witnesses had sworn to his being in Exchange Buildings. A fellow-lodger called Bekoff stated that neither he nor Duboff had left 20 Galloway Road after 8 p.m. on 16th December; they had gone to bed at 11.30. A friend named Schurig testified to having visited Duboff there that evening until after eleven o'clock. Mrs Petter, Duboff's landlady, confirmed that he had gone upstairs to bed at 11.30 and added that she had seen him again at breakfast next morning. She was sure he had never possessed a firearm or cartridges.

The evidence was overwhelmingly in favour of his clients, Maw told the bench, and they ought not to be put to the ordeal, nor the country to the expense, of trial. He had made up his mind to commit all four remaining prisoners, Treloar answered. Vassileva's counsel had already reserved her defence until the trial, and Arthur Bryan, newly-appointed counsel for Rosen, now decided to do likewise. The magisterial process arrived at its twenty-fourth and final sitting on 4th April, 104 days after the first.

26. And Then There Were None

The Old Bailey trial before Mr Justice Grantham[1] began on Monday, 1st May, and lasted eleven days. The initial count of murder against Peters and Duboff proved much less durable. Soon after Bodkin's opening, his Lordship intervened to remark that it was one of constructive murder only; there was no direct evidence whatever that the two men had fired any shot or had even been with those who did, and he considered the prosecution would be wise to drop the charge. The jury returned a formal verdict of 'not guilty', and, after 128 days, Jacob Peters and Yourka Duboff were no longer in fear for their necks.

A count of accessory after the fact to Tucker's murder was then taken. This survived until first thing the following morning. Under cross-examination by J. B. Melville, counsel for Peters and Duboff, Isaac Levy produced a new twist to his meeting with the fugitives:

Mr Melville: "Did you run away?"—"No. I thought that they had been firing in the air. I was not frightened. I thought they were students out for a lark."

"Did you seriously think they were threatening you with the revolvers?"—"No."

The judge did not wait for cross-examination to be completed.

[1] Sir William Grantham was seventy-five years of age and had spent a third of his life as a High Court judge. A high-principled and deeply religious man with an enviable judicial reputation, he had been reported by the *Daily Telegraph* on 6th January as commenting that the men who died in Sidney Street were Socialists of the very worst type, men who did not acknowledge God or anything; he hoped the siege would be a warning to people not to disregard religion.

He would not allow any jury to find a verdict of guilty on such unsatisfactory testimony, he observed. It was in any case merely evidence of identification, which would not be corroborated. To prove either charge that Peters and Duboff were accessories after the fact, it would be necessary to show that they were the men who carried Morountzeff. There was some evidence, such as that of Vassileva's close friendship with Morountzeff, which confirmed Levy's identification of her to a certain extent, though none to show that she had any part in the shooting. Nor, assuming that the three prisoners had in fact been seen leaving the scene of the crime, could the prosecution show that they knew murder to have been committed. All in all, he considered the charge unsafe and that the Crown would not be justified in pursuing it.

The jury returned a second finding of 'not guilty'. Having carefully studied all the evidence, his Lordship told them, he firmly believed that the shooting had been done by Morountzeff and the two men who later died in Sidney Street. It was some satisfaction that all three had ''met their doom'', if not in the customary way. There was nothing to show that Peter the Painter was one of the murderers.

The final count of conspiracy was then taken. The retelling of the prosecution's story disclosed little new information. Defence counsel harped constantly on the absentees, particularly Peter the Painter. Isaac Gordon told Walter Stewart, Vassileva's counsel, that she had said to him one day that she did not understand why the police were looking for Peter; he was ''never in existence''. She meant by this that Peter was ''not among the lot'', Isaac explained. Detective Superintendent Ottaway agreed with Bryan that the published description of Fritz Svaars also fitted Rosen.

Vassileva had been in England four years, Ottaway said, and the police knew of nothing against her previously. Her father had been a chef at the Imperial Palace in St Petersburg, Stewart told the court. Isaac Gordon emphatically denied having been paid by the police for ''looking after'' her after visiting Arbour Square with her books and papers. These dealt with sedition in Russia; it would have been an offence to possess them there.

It would be clearly shown, Melville declared in opening Peters's and Duboff's defence, that there were four men at Exchange Buildings on the night of 16th December: Morountzeff, Josef, Fritz and Max. Peter the Painter, undoubtedly a man of superior station in life to the others, might or might not have been a member of the conspiracy, but he stayed at home that night. It was natural enough that other Eastern Europeans should have been drawn into the Grove Street colony and that Peters should have associated with Fritz, his own cousin, on arriving in London. After Exchange Buildings three of the men he had named died, and the other two fled. Peters and Duboff, however, stood their ground and continued living their regular lives; this was the distinction between the innocent and the guilty in this case.

He would be able to prove, Bryan stated, that Rosen was not in or near Exchange Buildings on any of the occasions alleged. His client bore a remarkable resemblance to Fritz Svaars, and this was a straightforward case of mistaken identity.

Giving evidence for the first time, Jacob Peters answered counsels' questions calmly and openly. Obviously he and his notorious first cousin were totally unalike in character and temperament. Fritz had taken him to his lodgings at 29 Great Garden Street (a turning out of the Whitechapel Road, later renamed Greatorex Street) when he came to England, he said, but he left because he found his cousin impossible to live with. They never visited one another's homes after that, though Peters did go twice to 59 Grove Street about a fortnight before the murders as he had had a letter saying that Fritz's mother was anxious about him. Peters was gently scathing about his late cousin's politics:

Mr Melville: "Was Fritz a Socialist?"

Witness (smiling): "He would have been a better friend with the Russian *gendarmes* than with the Socialists." (Laughter.)

Mr Bodkin (later, in cross-examination): "Did you describe Fritz as an Anarchist?"—"He knew nothing about Anarchism. He called himself an Anarchist."

The gist of Peters's own story follows:

I was born in Courland in 1886 and worked first on a farm, then as a grocer's assistant in Libau until 1905. I was later a dock labourer and a hand in a butter-factory. I joined the Lettish Social Democratic Party and did propaganda work amongst army personnel and work-people. This work, which was unpaid, led to my being brought before a court in Riga. After being imprisoned for eighteen months pending inquiries, I was tried and acquitted. This was in 1908. I returned home but heard later that the police were about to visit me again. I went to Germany and then on to Denmark and finally, in the autumn of 1909, came to London.

I gave my proper name where I lived but worked as a tailor's presser under the name of Jacob Colnin, because I had become secretary of the party's London branch and I knew that East End employers disliked organized workers. Party workers in Russia commonly use several names.

I might have seen Morountzeff but did not know him personally. I saw Peter the Painter once at Fritz's lodgings. I was never at the Jubilee Street club. I knew absolutely nothing about the conspiracy until afterwards.

He usually went straight home after work, Peters said, but sometimes called in at the Russian library. On 16th December he finished at 7.30 and waited an hour for his wages, arriving home about nine o'clock. He ate supper, set a mouse-trap, did some reading and went to bed at about midnight. He got up next morning at his usual time.

Asked by Bodkin whether he considered property to belong to the community, Peters replied firmly that Social Democrats did not believe that the proceeds of everyone's work should be shared. His witnesses followed. The principal witness next day was Yourka Duboff, who said his real name was Laiwin. The son of a small farmer, he had joined the Lettish Social Democratic Workmen's Federation and, after the uprising of 1905, at the age of nineteen, had been found guilty of agitating in Riga. His punishment was a whipping from the Cossacks and banishment. He left home in 1906 and lived in London and the United States before revisiting Riga in 1909.

This was in fact Duboff's fourth spell in London; during the other three he had lived in the East End. Returning from Switzerland in September 1910, he had worked as a painter at the Savoy Hotel until mid-October and with another firm from mid-

November until 12th December. He had never been in Exchange Buildings, he said, and knew nothing about the conspiracy. Fritz, whom he had met only occasionally, had told him he was an engineer. He had known Morountzeff for some time but only casually.

Born in Riga, Rosen had taken that name on coming to England in January 1909. He had seen Fritz on the stage, he said, and thought he was an actor. He too had never been in Exchange Buildings and had known nothing about the proposed robbery. His wife deposed to having been with him from 6 to 11 p.m. on 16th December. Fritz Svaars was understood to have favoured a cap, and several Crown witnesses had spoken of seeing Rosen with one on; she had never known her husband wear a cap, Mrs Rosen said.

Addressing the jury, Melville dismissed the identification-parades in which Peters and Duboff had been picked out from amongst Britons as a farce, although not consciously unfair. The sheet-anchor of the case against the two men had been their alleged presence in Exchange Buildings at the time of the murders, he declared, and that had gone.

Summing up, his Lordship censured Constable Martin and Isaac Levy. In his view, both might have shown greater courage and a stronger sense of duty; Martin ought to have seen who the men were that carried Morountzeff away, and Levy could surely have followed them without risking his life. He thought the police had done their best in the case and had certainly not acted unfairly to the prisoners.

For the first time, Vassileva's natural liveliness deserted her. She sat motionless, shoulders hunched and head bent, listening despondently. When the jury returned after less than half an hour and the three men hastened back into the dock to hear their verdict, she lingered. Her apprehension proved justified; they had found Peters, Duboff and Rosen not guilty and her guilty. Her fears about returning to Russia had not been lost on them, however; they hoped the judge would not recommend her deportation. A formal verdict was returned that she, Peters and Duboff were not guilty of the second accessory charge, and, to their delight, her three companions were freed.

Vassileva's counsel spoke of her in his plea in mitigation as a friendless political refugee, an industrious worker of good character who had fallen under the baleful domination of others. Passing sentence, Mr Justice Grantham gave no sign of having been softened. There could be no doubt about Vassileva's implication, he said, though he was quite willing to believe that she had no intention of adding murder to the crime of attempted safe-breaking. Morountzeff was about as desperate a man as had ever set foot on English soil, as also were Fritz and Josef. He would comply with the jury's wish as regards deportation, but the case was a very bad one: the prisoner would serve two years without hard labour.

A lonely figure by herself in the dock, Vassileva's last words to the court were defiant. She was innocent, she declared. "You find me guilty because I have lived with a man and you found him guilty; but it has not been proved."

Vassileva's appeal was heard by the Court of Criminal Appeal on 19th June, when Stewart argued before the Lord Chief Justice, Mr Justice Darling and Mr Justice Bankes that Mr Justice Grantham's summing-up had misdirected the jury on a number of points. There was no evidence consistent only with her guilt, Stewart claimed.

Giving judgment on 20th June, two days before the Coronation, the Lord Chief Justice said that there was no direct evidence of conspiracy against the appellant other than that she was at 11 Exchange Buildings with others who were there for an unlawful purpose and certain equipment which could be useful to burglars was brought there. Vassileva's presence in no. 11 did not constitute proof that she knew the purpose to which no. 9 was being put, and her untruthfulness afterwards could well have resulted from fear rather than guilt. In particular, it did seem that the learned judge should have asked the jury to consider whether she might have been living at no. 11 not as a conspirator but simply as a mistress. The court felt obliged to quash her conviction.

And so the last accused went free. What became of Yourka Duboff and John Rosen after they had exchanged the gloom of the Central Criminal Court for the hot afternoon sunshine in Old

Bailey on 12th May 1911 is unknown. Jacob Peters returned to Russia after the revolution and became a senior member of the Cheka.[2] Karl Hoffmann and Josef Fedoroff also disappeared from view. Vassileva was still living modestly in the East End half a century later. Luba Milstein went to the United States.

Rosie Trassjonsky's discharge at Guildhall hastened a progressive mental deterioration that apparently led to her early death. Already deprived at a stroke of her beloved Peter and the *ménage* in Grove Street that had meant so much to her, she had now been excluded even from sharing stoically in the consequences of what her friends had done. Lonely, wretched and without purpose, she succumbed to melancholia and became suicidal; only four weeks after leaving Holloway Prison she had to be put under restraint of another kind. She was admitted to Colney Hatch Asylum.

Rosie had become a charge to the parish within twelve months of entering the country and was thus liable to expulsion under the Aliens Act. On 3rd June 1911 Bow Street magistrates' court granted a certificate recommending her deportation as an alien pauper. Whether the Home Secretary actually made an expulsion order is unknown; in any event, the subject was too ill for it to be executed.

Mental illness was little understood at that time, and sympathy for its victims was rare. Reference was made at the Old Bailey to Rosie's having been "put into a madhouse". Lena Vassileva at least was not one to forget a favour; she visited the afflicted woman, and J. P. Eddy gave an account of a modest seasonal remembrance:

> Then, just prior to Christmas 1912, a small brown-paper parcel was sent anonymously to the police containing a perfumed sachet; to it was pinned a plain envelope, on the face of which was written:
>
> Xmas, 1912
>
> To the nurse who so kindly tended Carl Garstin (alias Gardstein) during his last hours.

The parcel was from Vassileva. It was duly sent on to the asylum and acknowledged by the medical superintendent there. "No

[2] The organization set up in post-1917 Russia to combat counter-revolutionary activities, later known as the Ogpu.

further communication was received," wrote Eddy in conclusion, "and no doubt is entertained that she died at the asylum."[3]

Police despondency at the escape of the only people they had been able to bring to court was no doubt tempered by the realization that an exceptionally complex and arduous case had at last run its course. The City of London acquainted the Metropolitan Police Commissioner with its high appreciation of his force's work on the case and voted gratuities from the City police fund for conspicuous service: Chief Superintendent Stark was awarded £50, Detective Superintendent Ottaway £40, Detective Inspector Wensley £25, Detective Chief Inspector Willis £12.10s, Detective Inspectors Thompson and Newell and Detective Sergeant Leeson £10 each and five others £5 each.[4]

Stark was later to become Assistant Commissioner and Thompson detective superintendent; Ottaway transferred to Military Intelligence. Nott-Bower reproduced in his memoirs a personal letter received from the DPP after the trial, commending the "intelligent and untiring zeal" shown by his officers in the face of "quite extraordinary" difficulties.[5]

The journey from the strange sounds reported by Max Weil's servant-girl to the Court of Criminal Appeal's decision had taken six months, a period during which it sometimes seemed that the three dead policemen had been lost sight of, buried not only literally under the soil but figuratively by the pressure and drama of later events. It is fitting that this record of the Exchange Buildings–Sidney Street affair should end by describing a memorial to them. In the autumn of 1911 a tall monument in pink granite was placed at the head of the two graves at the City of London Cemetery, where it stands today. Its inscription reads:

[3] *Op. cit.*, p. 31.

[4] This list, from *The Times* of 22nd June 1911, makes no mention of Superintendent Mulvaney, but there was another in Nott-Bower's memoirs that did. Nott-Bower gave no amounts.

[5] *Op. cit.*, p. 249.

Sacred to the Memory of Sergeants Charles Tucker, aged 47,
and Robert Bentley, aged 37, interred here

and Constable Walter Charles Choat, aged 34, interred at Byfleet

Members of the City of London Police Killed in the Execution of
their Duty While Endeavouring to Apprehend a Number of
Armed Burglars in Exchange Buildings, Cutler Street, E.C.
16th December 1910

In appreciation of their devotion to duty
this monument is erected by the
Police Committee
and by the
officers and constables
City of London Police Force

Faithful Unto Death

Author's Notes

The crimes in Exchange Buildings and Sidney Street offer exceptional scope for speculation. I have tried in this book to provide the material needed to enable the reader to theorize for himself in any direction he may wish, rather than conclude with an ambitious—and no doubt voluminous—attempt to do so for him. Nevertheless, some personal observations may prove helpful.

The affray in Exchange Buildings was so unexpected, so quickly done and so deeply shocking for those innocently involved that one cannot hope to reconstruct it in close detail from the subsequent eye-witness accounts of it. The following seems to me a fair summary of what must have happened.

Whilst Max Smoller, recruited as a mechanic to assist in breaching the rear wall of 119 Houndsditch and assaulting Harris's safe, was engaged on the former, and Morountzeff hovered between nos. 9 and 11, Josef kept watch in one tenement and Fritz in the other. Which, then, was in which? Since Inspector Bryant identified Morountzeff as the man who rushed into no. 11's parlour from the backyard, and Constable Martin identified him (obviously wrongly) as the man who opened the door to Sergeant Bentley, it is reasonable to infer that these two men were fundamentally alike. The fact that Morountzeff and Josef were both tallish and dark, while Fritz was shorter and fair, strongly suggests that the man in no. 11 was Josef. We know too that Josef was the only one of Morountzeff's accomplices on intimate terms with him; holding the fort in no. 11, the tenement known to be occupied, was a special responsibility, and Morountzeff would be likely to choose him for it.

According to Martin, Josef disappeared behind the street door after Bentley had questioned him, apparently going upstairs;

about a minute then elapsed before Morountzeff came rushing in. The explanation for this hiatus undoubtedly lies in the window on the staircase between the first and second floors, looking out on the backyard; half an hour later, in spite of the windy December night, Superintendent Ottaway found it open. Josef raised the alarm from there and ran down to resume his position on the stairs.

It is perhaps not surprising that a burglar who accepts commitment to a plan which involves making a great deal of noise when the neighbourhood is at its quietest, and who fails to abandon that plan even when under the eye of the police, should rely on shooting his way out of the consequences with an unsuitable firearm which he cannot handle competently. Ideal as a Mauser might have been for impressing friends and overawing roughs, it was designed for long-range work rather than point-blank in-fighting. While Morountzeff was approaching Bentley and disposing of him with two deadly shots from his little Dreyse, Josef could only manage to put a bullet through the sergeant's helmet. One of his two wild shots into the parlour ceiling passed right through the bed in the room above—a salutary experience for Vassileva if she was nearby at the time.

When the shooting began, Bryant said, Bentley was standing in the parlour doorway, and he himself had stepped off the pavement into the passage. This being so, Bryant's left side is likely to have been concealed from Josef by the partly open street door and his right side from Morountzeff because Bentley was half on his right and half in front of him. As Bryant was wounded well over on his left side, the odds are that Morountzeff was also responsible for this. Bryant probably owed his life to being partially masked from Morountzeff at the crucial moment. Also, Bryant was aware of Josef's presence; if it had been Josef who shot him, he surely could have said afterwards whether Josef had fired or not.

Though obstructed by the fallen Bentley, the street doorway was now cleared of resistance. Josef reached it first and, firing through it with his arm extended (all Martin and Strongman could see of him was his hand), shot Woodhams. Morountzeff next passed through the doorway and, advancing a few steps towards Cutler Street, put paid to Sergeant Tucker. Choat, probably standing in the shadows across the carriageway, remained unseen. Needing to reload, and considering it safe to bring Vassileva out, Morountzeff then turned and went back into no. 11. Josef meanwhile had continued blazing away from the doorway behind him, and, as Morountzeff came up to him, no doubt the two exchanged a few words; at all events, Josef now took to his heels and fled into Cutler Street. Several witnesses spoke of seeing this first lone fugitive; watching from no. 5, Bessie Jacobs thought he was the man who had just been shooting at Tucker.

No. 9 was in darkness all this time, and no one paid any attention to it. At about the moment that Morountzeff re-entered no. 11, Fritz and Max decided to quit the other tenement. Both had their pistols at the ready. Choat approached Fritz at once, closed with him and, as the smaller man struggled desperately to free himself, received a Mauser bullet in the loin and three more in his left leg. Three things now happened more or less simultaneously: Choat's left leg crumpled under him, and he fell; Morountzeff rushed up and bent over him to deliver the *coup de grâce*—two Dreyse bullets in the back; and in the confusion Max accidentally shot his leader. When Harry Jacobs said he saw a second man run out of no. 11 and fire at Choat's back, he was almost certainly referring to Morountzeff's second sortie out of no. 11.

Supporting Morountzeff between them and followed at a discreet distance by his distraught mistress, Fritz and Max then beat as hasty a retreat as they could. At the entrance to Borer's Passage, Isaac Levy came face to face with them and was shaken off. When they turned into Harrow Alley, Josef rejoined them, and Vassileva was told to make herself scarce; by the time the two council contractor's employees saw the party, it had thus become four men.

Grove Street, only about half as far from Exchange Buildings as Gold Street, was the nearest refuge; it was decided to deposit Morountzeff at no. 59. The journey was probably no more hazardous than strenuous, the East End streets being full of stir and bustle at that hour and the sight of a helpless drunk being escorted home by his friends a common enough one. During the hurried final arrangements at no. 59, Morountzeff handed over his key to 44 Gold Street.

There is only Isaac Levy's evidence to show that Vassileva was still in Exchange Buildings when the affray occurred. However, if we assume that she left earlier, as she told Isaac Gordon and John Rosen she had, we must also assume that Levy invented the woman he described as accompanying the escaping party. Misidentification is one thing but such a pointless flight of fancy quite another; Levy must really have seen this woman, and she must really have been Vassileva.

Max's blunder (and Choat's extreme bravery) not only provided next day's vital lead into the case but removed a deadly enemy; the length of the police casualty-list, if Morountzeff too had been cornered and confronted in Sidney Street style, can be readily imagined.

In the minds of public and police alike, Morountzeff's skill and determination as a policemen's executioner rubbed off on Josef and Fritz. The dubious distinction was undeserved. To me this oddly inefficient, excitable pair emerge from the story as actors in a series of charades, no more intent on the lawless deeds they performed than on the image of themselves which performing those deeds would create, like adolescents claiming manhood. Reckless and ruthless as he undoubtedly was, Morountzeff at least meant what he did and did what he meant.

Looked at in this light, there is considerable pathos in the lives of these two delinquents and the perverted heroism of their last hours. A comparison of their behaviour in Sidney Street with that of Hefeld and Meyer in the 'Tottenham Outrage' (see Appendix) reveals several interesting similarities. A number of possible reasons for the onset of such frenzy under such circumstances have been suggested to me, one of the more intriguing being the practice in these men's infancy of swaddling babies so tightly that they could not kick. In any event, it is hardly surprising that young men who have learned from the cradle that authority will assert itself arbitrarily, inexorably and often brutally should lash out blindly when they find themselves trapped by it. The trage-dies of Tottenham, Exchange Buildings and Sidney Street came about because the sins of the old, malevolent authority were visited upon the new, benevolent one.

Frantic behaviour apart, a popular theory of the time held that alien desperadoes like Morountzeff carried firearms for fear not of arrest itself but of subsequent deportation. Lena Vassileva's dread was common to hundreds of Eastern European immigrants.

It seems eminently reasonable to call a man an Anarchist when he is shown not only to have held Anarchist convictions but to have acted upon them, whether as terrorist, murderer, thief or in any other capacity; and the City Police were surely justified, therefore, in maintaining that Morountzeff was one. No doubt he planned to leave for the Continent immediately after the robbery, taking some of the stolen property with him to hand over to the organization he was associated with. It is interesting to note that the headquarters of the international bureau which the orthodox Anarchist movement decided in 1907 to set up to facilitate liaison between its different groups were in Stepney Green—only a stone's throw from Morountzeff's lodgings in Gold Street.

Mention of the Sidney Street siege brings two words to most people's minds: Churchill and Anarchists. The reader will have formed his own opinions about the former's attendance. Many years afterwards, Randolph Churchill was to admit on his father's behalf that "Churchill himself in later life felt that perhaps he should not have yielded to his 'curiosity' by going to Sidney Street".[1] The inverted commas around the word curiosity are Randolph's. Curiosity may have brought about his presence, but it fails to explain much of his surprising behaviour there.

The Anarchist legend brought the men who died in no. 100 a kind of canonization in some anti-authoritarian circles. However, this was almost certainly one of the areas in which Fritz Svaars and Josef Sokoloff were masqueraders. "He knew nothing about Anarchism," said Jacob Peters of his cousin at the Old Bailey; "he called himself an Anarchist." Their personal friend concluded that both men used Anarchism as a cover. There are other good

---

[1] Randolph S. Churchill, *Winston S. Churchill*: Volume II, *Young Statesman, 1901–14* (Heinemann, 1966), p. 409.

reasons, including Scotland Yard's categorical statement of 6th January, for believing that the pair were really only thieves in Anarchist clothing.

The thought of Fritz poring over political ideologies (as his naturally earnest and studious cousin must certainly have done) and becoming converted to Anarchism is incongruous, to say the least; it is unlikely that such a man would even possess the mental capacity to do so. One knows less of Josef, but I think both men were desperadoes of the type that Morountzeff was reported to have gathered round him in Warsaw, of negligible intellect and exclusively, or at any rate primarily, interested in personal profit. No doubt the two men considered that this pretence of political motivation flattered them and—as many other Continental villains had done—found it useful in their trade.

Amongst those who supported the notion (disdained by both London police forces) that Peter the Painter was a Russian Government agent were Ramsay MacDonald, actor Laurence Irving, author Gerald Bullett and many of the Russian colony in London. This theory was never widely held, however, and the motives of most of its adherents must be regarded as suspect; embarrassed compatriots of the criminals, for example, found it especially handy, suggesting as it did that they were babes in the wood who had been sinned against rather than sinning. It cannot have been much less convenient for MacDonald with his deep-seated distrust of policemen and passionate concern for the welfare of any foreigner whatsoever whom he considered downtrodden. Irving, who had many Russian *émigré* friends, admitted having got the idea from them, and Bullett appears to have seized on it purely as a tasty morsel for his short account of the Exchange Buildings case already referred to. He wrote in this of a certain amount of corroborative evidence for the theory but omitted to put any of it on record; nor am I aware of anyone else ever doing so.

In considering this hypothesis and the parallel one that, although not an *agent provocateur*, Peter the Painter was nevertheless responsible for the whole affair, at least four awkward questions arise. First of all, can either be reconciled with the Painter's close contact in London being not Morountzeff, or even

Josef, but Fritz? There is nothing whatever to suggest that he had any special relationship with Morountzeff such as both theories require. Vassileva, who had actually kept house for her lover during much of the material time, told her landlord afterwards that she could not understand why the police were looking for the Painter. Moreover, it is as difficult to believe that Morountzeff, a self-orientated extremist of no small intelligence and an experienced leader in his own right, would suddenly surrender himself to the newcomer's initiative as it is to understand how and when this was exercised.

Secondly, is it reasonable to suppose that Morountzeff and his accomplices were under the domination of a man not even present when the robbery was attempted? Such a situation is quite possible nowadays, but the Exchange Buildings affair occurred many years before the advent of modern highly organized crime. Thirdly, if Peter the Painter was indeed the ringleader, what was the point of his simultaneously finding himself a good job as a house-painter? An *agent provocateur* who had deliberately set up a flawed plan for the robbery would surely have prepared to disappear after its discovery, and a straightforward leader expecting his plan to succeed would have had his share of the spoils to look forward to. The final question concerns his behaviour after the catastrophe on the night of 16th December: was this what might be expected of a Russian Government agent? He fled with the others to 36 Lindley Street and—unlike Max—showed no desire to keep away from them and their friends.

None of these points defy argument, but their cumulative force is formidable. That the Painter helped plan the intended robbery is a distinct possibility; but this is a very different matter from master-minding the enterprise. I myself see him as what was called in those days an 'Anarchist of the study', an amiable, cultured individual with a social conscience and a taste for the company of ruffians, whose worth as a status-lender Fritz of all people would not have been slow to appreciate; this would account for Peter's presence at 59 Grove Street, his having the better room there all to himself and never being called upon to pay the rent, among other things. To be fair to Fritz, he was probably stimulating company for the Painter, besides lending *him* status of a sort he enjoyed seeming to have.

The law may not have found the eight who answered to it guilty, but the City Police Commissioner had no hesitation in doing so. In his memoirs Nott-Bower lumped them in with the five who had died or escaped abroad, described all thirteen as "this criminal gang"[2] and recorded their eventual release with considerable bitterness. This outcome, he remarked, would have been comic if not so unfortunate: "English law maintained its great traditions, and the criminals went free." He also stigmatized the "persons of the very lowest type . . . none having the smallest regard for truth"[3] from whom evidence had had to be obtained, people who viewed the police with suspicion and were reluctant to co-operate, reneged on their statements, knew no English and so forth. Wensley echoed these criticisms, though more philosophically, five years later in *his* memoirs.

It requires no great skill at reading between the lines to detect the Commissioner's chagrin at the indifferent results the police had produced. As Wensley himself admitted, the prosecution evidence "proved little beyond the fact that [the accused] were associated with each other and with the murderers".[4] The reader will have reached his own conclusions as to the accuseds' guilt or innocence; I myself am convinced that—Vassileva apart—their release was really due not so much to the type of person from whom evidence had to be gathered, or to the tenderness of English law towards foreigners (as Wensley put it, and Blackstone before him), as to their innocence of the charges brought against them. Behind the proceedings against them, in fact, one can sense an ugly resolve to make the accessible outside group the scapegoat for the misdeeds of the inaccessible inside one.

Symptoms of this attitude are plentiful enough. To select only two: what possible justification can there have been for charging

---

[2] *Op. cit.*, p. 231. He listed Max Smoller and Joe Levi as two different people. However, Donald Rumbelow wrote (*op. cit.*) of them as having been the same man, and my information strongly suggests that they were.

[3] *Op. cit.*, p. 247 (also the previous quotation).

[4] *Op. cit.*, p. 166.

Fedoroff with murder? And surely the uncorroborated identification of Peters and Duboff by such a palpably unreliable person as Isaac Levy should have been recognized as inadequate to sustain a murder charge long before Mr Justice Grantham so forthrightly rejected it? As has already been recorded, cases conducted by the DPP were not uncommonly disfigured by such vindictiveness. It certainly cannot be laid at the door of the City Police, who were only his instruments. Allowing for the rough-and-ready police methods of those days, the City force's conduct towards the accused—humble immigrants associated with the murderer of their colleagues—seems to have been in the best traditions of the British police.

In spite of Nott-Bower's and Wensley's admissions that the information in police possession had come from extremely unsatisfactory sources, both drew a distinction between what could be given in evidence against the prisoners and what was known to the police. "No attempt was made to produce anything but the strictest legal evidence against them," Wensley wrote.[5] This strikes me as pure innuendo, intended to persuade us that the difference would have tipped the scales decisively against them. If any such additional, vital *knowledge* in support of the charges had existed, such a determined prosecutor as the DPP would surely have contrived to introduce relative evidence of some kind and get it admitted.

Writing about the case nearly half a century after Nott-Bower, my friend Donald Rumbelow of the City Police[6] abandoned the traditional interpretation of events and put forward Jacob Peters as the Exchange Buildings killer. I found his arguments extremely interesting but, alas, unconvincing. Two major points in refutation may be made here.

First, as to character. The ferocious efficiency of the Exchange Buildings killings was entirely consistent with Morountzeff's past record and entirely inconsistent with Peters's, which had to do solely with making seditious propaganda. Furthermore, the Lettish Social Democrats in London had considered Peters level-

[5] *Op. cit.*, p. 166.

[6] *Op. cit.*

headed and responsible enough to elect him their branch secretary; he was in fact a dedicated political moderate who had found his cousin's attitudes intolerable and would certainly have steered well clear of any dealings whatever with an unbalanced extremist like Morountzeff. It will also be remembered that Peters was not at the Grove Street meeting on the afternoon of the murders; that he was not amongst the callers at either 35 New Castle Place or 36 Lindley Street; that he had an excellent record at work; that he stood his ground after the murders, both at work and where he lived; and that he did not offer the smallest resistance when detained.

Secondly, Inspector Bryant had actually stood beside Sergeant Bentley as Bentley's killer crossed the brightly lit parlour of no. 11 towards them firing his pistol. If this man had really been Peters, it is surely inconceivable that (as he did at Guildhall on 16th January 1911) Bryant could have positively identified him as Morountzeff—with Peters, charged with murder, sitting in the dock a few feet away from him as he did so. At the same sitting and also in Peters's presence, Constable Strongman identified Morountzeff as Tucker's murderer too.

The story is already very congested, and squeezing Peters right into the middle of it strains one's credulity in many other directions. For instance, out must go the natural explanation of the Dreyse found in the bedding under Morountzeff's pillow being his own and there for a last-ditch defence, also the natural sequence of Fritz and Josef possessing and using a Mauser apiece first in Exchange Buildings and later in Sidney Street. According to Rumbelow, Fritz and Josef were not even present in Exchange Buildings when the affray took place; his version has them sitting in the front room at 59 Grove Street all evening. If this were indeed so, can one really believe that they would later have fought to the death in no. 100 as they did?

And, finally, what was the evidence of Peters having been in Exchange Buildings at the time of the murders? Only Isaac Levy's identification of him. And Levy identified Duboff also—who, 5 miles away in his lodgings in Shepherd's Bush, had a cast-iron alibi. Personally, I am convinced that Levy's identification of the two men arose from an intense desire to restore his credit with the police after his initial failure to tell them about his meeting with the escaping party, and was entirely false. (This is not to say that he lied consciously and deliberately. I think he felt a desperate need for Peters and Duboff to have been the two men he had seen.)

Although for several good solid reasons it is the custom of men who plan robberies to keep the number of participants down to an absolute minimum, both Nott-Bower and Rumbelow wrote of a whole platoon of active confederates. There are a great many inconsistencies and loose ends, of course, which are unlikely now ever to be satisfactorily explained. Was Betsy Gershon's vital evidence regarding Josef Sokoloff the reason she did not have to face accessory charges such as those brought against Luba Milstein? After the prosecution had paraded its witnesses— many of them patently unreliable—to all the accused except Luba and Karl Hoffmann having frequented Exchange Buildings, why did the defence not capitalize on the fact that only Vassileva's fingerprints were found? How can the police descriptions of Peter the Painter's shabbiness be reconciled with several people considering him exceptionally well-dressed?

And so on and so on. But our indigenous real-life crimes seldom come in the neat packages of the fictitious kind; and this exotic affair was untidier even than them.

Appendix   'The Tottenham Outrage'

On Saturday morning, 23rd January 1909, a firm of india-rubber-cover repairers called Schnurmann's sent a young clerk in a motor-car from its premises in Chesnut Road, Tottenham, to the bank to draw the week's wages. The money, £80, was all in coins; the clerk, whose name was Keyworth, returned at 9.30 with it in a canvas bag. As he started to cross the pavement to the factory entrance, two men named Paul Hefeld (or Hegeld) and Jacob Meyer (or Lapidus) rushed at him and snatched the bag. Both produced pistols, and the chauffeur was fired on when he tried to intervene, one bullet knocking off his cap. They then took to their heels, followed by several passers-by.

The nearest police-station was less than fifty yards away. Constables Tyler and Newman (one of whom left it through a window) at once dashed to the motor-car, clambered in with the chauffeur and set out after them. The two fugitives, who had plenty more ammunition in their pockets, turned at intervals to fire at their pursuers and had soon wounded one of them in the head. When Hefeld noticed that the motor-car was gaining on them, he stopped, aimed carefully and put it out of action with a stream of shots, one smashing the windscreen and another holing the radiator. The two policemen leaped out and carried on on foot.

The chase north-eastwards continued. Attracted by the uproar, a ten-year-old boy called Ralph Joscelyn ran into the narrowing gap between pursuers and pursued and was shot dead. When only a few yards behind the thieves, Constable Tyler called out "Give it up! The game is over!" Hefeld again halted, sighted his pistol coolly and fired; Tyler was hit in the neck and temple and died almost immediately. Constable Newman, himself bleeding from a cheek-wound, broke off to attend to his colleague.

As the pursuit went on, its numbers grew. Horses, horses and carts, motor-cars and bicycles were pressed into service. In response to alarm calls throughout the area, large numbers of police began to close in on the fugitives' anticipated route. An omnibus was commandeered and filled with policemen. Those who had been issued with revolvers returned the thieves' fire, as also did some sportsmen with shot-guns and a few other armed civilians. Of their quarry, Hefeld was clearly the better marksman; Meyer's main contribution was to reload one pistol while he fired the other. The list of casualties lengthened.

On reaching the Chingford Road in Walthamstow, over 2 miles from Chesnut Road, the two men held up an electric tram-car and climbed on board. Suddenly aware of whistling bullets, the driver fled upstairs to the top deck. Meyer marched the conductor, a man named Wyatt, through the tram-car. The door to the driver's platform was locked, but Wyatt dared not hesitate; he smashed the glass panel, and they went through. With Meyer's pistol sometimes brushing his cheek and Hefeld on the rear platform firing periodic bursts at the following crowd, Wyatt drove the squealing, shuddering vehicle south for about half a mile as fast as it would go.

There were only three other passengers. Two of them, a young woman and her child, cowered together on the floor. The third, an elderly man called Loveday, tried to come to Wyatt's assistance and was shot in the throat. A tram-car travelling towards them reached a loop line in the nick of time. Behind them a tram-car which had come up soon after the departure of Wyatt's was packed with about forty policemen and others and sent off in hot pursuit, accompanied by a private motor-car and several mounted police. Other policemen who took to a bill-poster's pony-and-trap were tipped unceremoniously into the road when a bullet felled the animal.

Wyatt's tram-car having finally been forced to a halt, the thieves abandoned it, shot and wounded a milkman and made off at a gallop in his float. They were by now almost at Tower Hamlet, but their luck began to fail. The float careered into a wall, and when they seized a greengrocer's cart, they discovered it had its chain-brake on. A race across fields with the huge, excited crowd strung out behind them took them into a cul-de-sac bounded by a stout 6-foot fence topped with barbed wire.

Dishevelled, bleeding and struggling desperately for breath, Meyer managed to scramble over, but his partner was exhausted. As a police sergeant on a bicycle came up to him, Hefeld shot himself in the forehead. The injury was not immediately fatal.

Meyer got little further, finding a last temporary refuge in Oak Hill Cottage, Hale End, the four-roomed home of a coalman called Rolstone and his family. Eliza Rolstone heard all the commotion and came out of the front of the house with her youngest child in her arms as the hunted man went in at the rear. Told to go back inside because a murderer was loose, she started to do so but caught sight of Meyer's face staring out at her. Her two other children were still in the house; a young man whose identity was never discovered managed to bring them out.

Not the least remarkable feature of the affair was Meyer's behaviour on finding himself cornered. He first tried to hide himself in the kitchen chimney; finding it too small, he then rushed upstairs to the front bedroom, where his appearance at the window was greeted with several bullets. Three armed policemen, Constables Eagles and Cater and Detective Constable Dixon, went into the house after him; Dixon later described him as "tearing about the room" and "laughing wildly". He yelled "Come on now!" at the constables, flung himself on a child's bed that was near the window and tried to conceal himself under the bedclothes. When Eagles and Dixon charged in and disarmed him, they found him severely wounded. They dragged him downstairs and into the yard, and as he lay there between life and death, the crowd surged in to look at him. There was "a horrible grin" on his face, Dixon said, "an awful look" which remained fixed until he died.

The chase had covered about five miles and lasted an hour and a half; two men and a boy were dead and sixteen others injured. A number of bullets which had been fired into the bedroom through the window and through and round the door could have caused Meyer's death; being about an inch in front of the top of his right ear, his principal gunshot wound could also have been self-inflicted. Invited to choose between verdicts of justifiable homicide and *felo de se*, the inquest jury decided on the latter.

Hefeld died on 12th February. The police had learned little from him except that he, and probably Meyer also, came from the Baltic province of Riga. Both men were in their early twenties; although both had revolutionary connections, the robbery was thought to have been committed solely for personal profit. Hefeld had recently worked at Schnurmann's and would have been familiar with the wages routine on Saturday mornings.

Eagles, Cater and Dixon were all awarded the King's Police Medal. The stolen money was never recovered. Concern was expressed at the inquests about the "alien threat" and the short-comings of the Aliens Act, but this aspect attracted no great attention.

Index

n = footnote